THE PARISH COUNCIL HANDBOOK

for old and new members

ANGLICAN DIOCESE OF MELBOURNE

THE RT REVD DR BRADLY S BILLINGS

Edited by Dr Ian Gibson, the Advocate
With a foreword by Mr Ken Spackman, the Registrar

The Parish Council Handbook
for old and new members
First edition

First published in 2017
by the Anglican Diocese of Melbourne
The Anglican Centre
209 Flinders Lane
Melbourne VIC 3000

Copyright © Anglican Diocese of Melbourne 2016

All rights reserved. No part of this publication may be reproduced, stored in a retrieval system or transmitted, in any form or by any means electronic, photocopying, recording or otherwise, without the prior written permission of the publisher.

Produced for the Anglican Diocese of Melbourne
by Broughton Publishing Pty Ltd
32 Glenvale Crescent
Mulgrave VIC 3170

ISBN: 978-0-9806634-2-6

Contents

Foreword 2
1. The Parish 5
2. The Council 11
3. Composition of the Parish Council 15
4. Functions of the Parish Council 25
5. Communications and Representation 35
6. Other Committees, Groups or Teams 37
7. Prayer 40
8. Consulting Together 42
9. Preparing for the Meeting 48
10. What Happens at a Parish Council Meeting? 51
11. The Annual Meeting 57
12. Through the Year 65
13. When the Vicar Leaves 69

Appendices

One—Glossary 71
Two—A Treasury of Prayers 79
Three—Further Resources 94
Four—The Parish Governance Act 2013 97
    Schedule 1. Parish rules for meetings and officers 172
    Parish Governance Regulations 2014 203

Foreword

The Anglican Church has a long history of shared governance, both in the context of the parish and, of course, in the Synod, in which the ordained leadership of the church acts in consultation and cooperation with the laity, for the corporate good and the advancement of God's kingdom.

This useful handbook has been prepared for those who presently take part in the significant responsibility of parish governance by serving as a member of a parish council; and, equally and importantly, for those who may be considering doing so, either now or at a future time. It will also be useful for those who may have, or who have been invited to, put their name forward for parish council, and would like to know what they might be in for!

The handbook is intended to be a practical resource, and for this reason not only covers the details of parish governance as set out by the *Parish Governance Act 2013*, but also contains a glossary of common terms and a treasury of prayers for a range of occasions, for use by both individuals and parish council. The full text of the *Parish Governance Act 2013*, together with the rules for meetings and officers and the regulations, are also included in the appendices for ease of reference.

The handbook has been written and prepared by Bishop Bradly Billings, who was chair of the parish legislation review committee that drafted the *Parish Governance Act 2013* and presented it to the Synod in 2013. Bishop Billings (then an Archdeacon) moved the motion to adopt the new Act, which I was pleased to second. The motion was accepted on the final day of that year's session of Synod, with considerable acclaim.

Bishop Billings has been vicar of two parishes (Gisborne and Toorak), an Archdeacon, and is presently the Director of Theological Education and Clergy Wellbeing for the diocese. He has extensive experience in corporate governance, having served previously on two school boards, for several years as a director of Benetas (Anglican Aged Care), and more recently as the Chair and Executive Officer of the Melbourne Anglican Foundation.

The Advocate, Dr Ian Gibson, who substantially drafted the *Parish Governance Act 2013*, applied his considerable expertise and attention to detail in editing the work, suggesting several improvements to the text and clarifying many matters of importance.

Both Bishop Billings and Dr Gibson are extremely well placed, and well qualified, for the task of producing this helpful and concise guide to parish governance for Anglicans in the Diocese of Melbourne.

I commend this useful and accessible handbook to the wider diocese, confident that it will be a blessing and benefit to parish councils everywhere.

Ken A. Spackman
Registrar

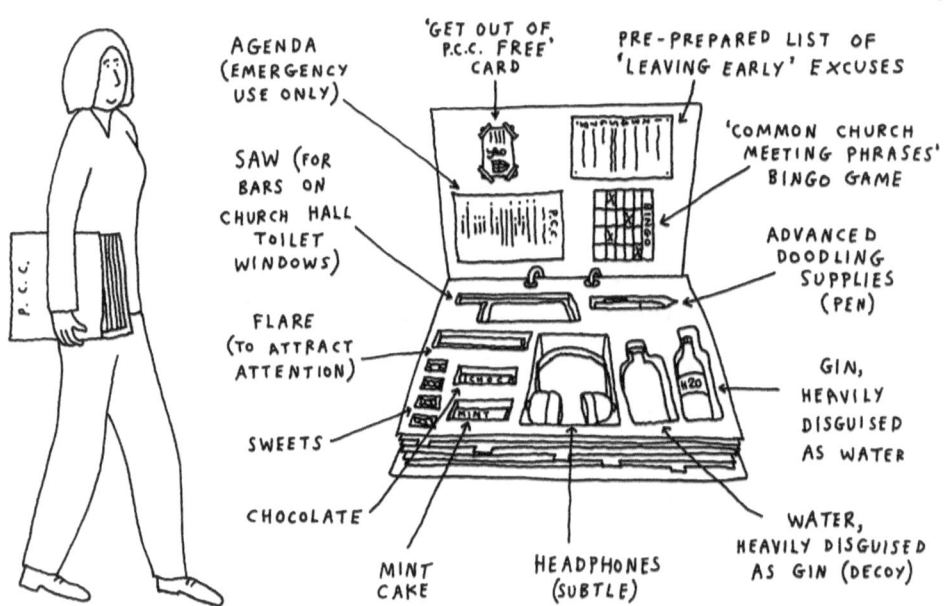

1. The Parish

The Anglican Diocese of Melbourne has in the recent past, as part of its strategic vision and directions, invited its people to 'see the parish with fresh eyes'. This entailed doing things such as gathering data on who lives in the community, the various activities that take place, and the different groups and organisations present. One suggestion that accompanied the invitation to 'see the parish with fresh eyes' was that parishioners take a walk around the surrounding streets and into the shopping centres and other places where people gather, and prayerfully observe the nature of the community. This points to the Anglican understanding of the parish. It refers to a locality, a geographical area, in which, of course, people live, work, study, fellowship and form community. Not all ministry is conducted in a parish setting—there are ministries to school communities, to workplaces, prisons, hospitals, aged care facilities, to the defence forces and emergency services, and many others. But all ministry, including parish ministry, does take place in the context of a community, however those communities are constituted, and whatever their size and composition.

This handbook is about parish ministry and, more particularly, about the parish council. So we begin with two fundamental questions. In this chapter the question, 'What is a parish?' and in the second chapter, 'What is a council?' They point to the overarching question we are attempting to answer in this handbook, which concerns what happens when those two words, 'parish' and 'council', come together.

Happily, in relation to our first question, the *Parish Governance*

Act 2013 section 5 provides a helpful definition. Under the subtitle 'The Anglican understanding of a parish', it reads—

> The parish is the geographical unit for organising the mission of God throughout the Anglican Church within the Diocese of Melbourne. The boundaries of each parish are those approved by the Archbishop in Council. The Anglican Church within the Diocese is constituted of clergy and lay people committed to building up the Body of Christ under the leadership of the Archbishop.
>
> This definition tells us some things of particular importance—
>
> - That the parish is a geographical area (or unit). This means that each parish is especially responsible, in terms of its mission and ministry, for the community or communities within those boundaries (but, importantly, not necessarily for more than this).
> - The purpose of organising the diocese into parishes is to facilitate the mission of God. This is, fundamentally, why the parish exists, and why there is one or more places of worship within it—to live out the call to mission that Jesus gave to his Church (Matthew 28.19–20). This is also primarily why the parish has a council, but more on that later.
> - The boundaries of each parish are not randomly constituted, nor determined at our own whim or desire, but are those approved by the Archbishop in Council. This alerts us to the fact that all parishes, and all parish councils, work within the confines of the broader structures of the church, such as the Archbishop in Council, and the Synod.
> - The Anglican Church, we learn, is made up of clergy and laypeople that are committed to building up the Body of Christ. That is, to further enhancing, growing and building this Anglican part of the wider Christian family. The parish, and the parish council, have an important role to play in this.

In fact, it is not too much to say that this is a large and important reason that the parish council exists!

- Finally, all of this is done under the leadership of the Archbishop. Because the Anglican Church is an episcopal church (led by bishops), both the diocese as a whole, and the parishes within it, can be thought as being 'gathered' around their chief pastor and leader—in the case of Melbourne, this is the Archbishop.

This tells us quite a bit about the meaning and purpose of the parish, and how it relates to the diocese in which it is located. It is worth noting, at this point, that the parish is the smallest unit of organisation within the Anglican Church. It is, therefore, inherently 'local.' For this reason, the name of each parish will normally include the place in which it is physically located. The parish is, however, not the only unit making up the whole of the church, but is one part within a much larger whole.

There is, for example, a parish of Malvern (St George's), which has particular responsibility for Anglican ministry in the inner south-eastern suburb of Malvern. The parish of Malvern is one small part of a much larger whole, which can be described in the following way—

i. The parish of Malvern is included in the deanery of Stonnington, which includes eight other parishes in the same part of Melbourne. The clergy and authorised lay ministers who are licensed to the parishes of the deanery meet together regularly for mutual prayer, support and encouragement.

ii. The deanery of Stonnington is within the archdeaconry of Stonnington and Glen Eira, whose Archdeacon also has administrative and missional responsibilities and duties for both the Stonnington deanery and the neighbouring deanery of Glen Eira.

iii. The parish of Malvern, the deanery of Stonnington, and the archdeaconry of Stonnington and Glen Eira, are each within

iv.   one of the three areas of episcopal care overseen by an assistant bishop.

iv.   The Diocese of Melbourne is, in turn, one diocese in the ecclesiastical province of Victoria, which also includes, in addition to Melbourne, the dioceses of Ballarat, Bendigo, Gippsland and Wangaratta.

v.   The Diocese of Melbourne is one diocese among the 23 individual dioceses that make up the Anglican Church of Australia.

vi.   The Anglican Church of Australia is, in turn, one part of the worldwide Anglican Communion, made up of those national churches having their historic origins in the Church of England.

vii.   The worldwide Anglican Communion is itself a part of the one, holy, catholic and apostolic church that stretches back in time all the way to Jesus and the first apostles, and which continues to exist today in a variety of forms and expressions across the globe.

Hence, we can understand the parish to be one part of the universal Christian church: a small, but important, part in the context of that larger whole. Furthermore, the nature of the parishes we are concerned with in this book are units within the Anglican Church, and a part of the Anglican Diocese of Melbourne. As such, the parish, through its clergy and its laypeople, is shaped and informed by the history and traditions, and the faith and practice, of the Anglican Church. This inevitably invites the question of what form the history and traditions take, and of what the content and particularities of the faith and practice might be. Here, the constitution of the Anglican Church of Australia is refreshingly helpful, for it sets out, in its fundamental declarations, a helpful summary of how the Anglican Church understands itself within the broader context of the worldwide

Christian church, and in the light of its own history and traditions, together with the sources of its faith and practice.

The 'fundamental declarations' (sections 1, 2 and 3) of the constitution of the Anglican Church of Australia, are—

1. The Anglican Church of Australia, being a part of the One Holy Catholic and Apostolic Church of Christ, holds the Christian Faith as professed by the Church of Christ from primitive times and in particular as set forth in the creeds known as the Nicene Creed and the Apostles' Creed.
2. This Church receives all the canonical scriptures of the Old and New Testaments as being the ultimate rule and standard of faith given by inspiration of God and containing all things necessary for salvation.
3. This Church will ever obey the commands of Christ, teach His doctrine, administer His sacraments of Holy Baptism and Holy Communion, follow and uphold His discipline and preserve the three orders of bishops, priests and deacons in the sacred ministry.

The 'ruling principles' (section 4) further state—

4. This Church, being derived from the Church of England, retains and approves the doctrine and principles of the Church of England embodied in the Book of Common Prayer together with the Form and Manner of Making Ordaining and Consecrating of Bishops, Priests and Deacons and in the Articles of Religion sometimes called the Thirty-nine Articles.

This gives us a helpful overview of the Anglican understanding of the parish in the context of the larger whole of the Christian church, and of its purpose in terms of what it is called to do and proclaim. It reminds us that the parish is a missional unit. Those who make up the people of God in that particular place are a sign, and hopefully a visible and active sign, of the presence of God in the midst of that community. As Teresa of Avila (1515–1582) so beautifully put it—

>Christ has no body but yours,
>No hands, no feet on earth but yours,
>Yours are the eyes with which he looks
>Compassion on this world,
>Yours are the feet with which he walks to do good,
>Yours are the hands, with which he blesses all the world.
>Yours are the hands, yours are the feet,
>Yours are the eyes, you are his body.
>Christ has no body now but yours,
>No hands, no feet on earth but yours,
>Yours are the eyes with which he looks
>Compassion on this world.
>Christ has no body now on earth but yours.

2. The Council

The parish council has its origins in the way the Church of England organised itself from the sixteenth century onwards. At that time the body responsible for governing the affairs of the geographical area of the parish was called a vestry, as it often met in the church vestry (the room in a church where the clergy robe, or 'vest', before a service of worship). For centuries, in England, the vestry had charge of both church related, or ecclesiastical, and civic affairs for everyone who lived in the parish area, whether they attended the church or not. In England, this terminology was changed in 1919 when the Parochial Church Council, or PCC, replaced the vestry as the governing body within the Church of England.[1]

In the Diocese of Melbourne the old term 'vestry' continued to be used for what is now the parish council, right up until the adoption of the *Parish Governance Act 2013* at the 2013 session of Synod.

The Diocese of Melbourne has historically understood itself to be 'episcopally led', that is led by bishops, and 'synodically governed', in that a representative body of clergy and laypeople gather in the context of Synod to consult together and to vote on matters of importance to the life of the church. In a parish setting, this same principle finds expression in the form of the parish council, wherein the vicar of the parish shares leadership, decision making, and matters requiring general consultation and consensus, with the laypeople that make up the parish council.

---

1   Martin Davie, *A guide to the Church of England* (London: Bloomsbury, 2008), p. 47.

> ## Parish rules for meetings and officers
>
> The parish council is established by the parish rules for meetings and officers, which set out the procedure for calling and holding the annual meeting, and for the election and appointment of members of the parish council. Those responsible for governance in each parish need to be familiar with the parish rules for meetings and officers. Model rules are contained in a schedule to the Parish Governance Act. These are the default rules. Each parish may decide to modify them in certain ways permitted by the Act. If modified, the new set of rules must be lodged with the registrar and agreed to afresh at least every 10 years.
>
> **See further:** The parish rules for meetings and officers (Schedule 1 of the Parish Governance Act 2013) reproduced in Appendix Four.

It is important to understand that, whilst it may look like a board or council with various powers and functions, the parish council has as its primary focus the worship of Almighty God, and the advancement of the good news about His son Jesus Christ. The parish council is, corporately, a disciple and follower of Christ, as all Christians are individually. Whilst elections, motions, voting, and the very title 'council' suggest the parish council has some of the powers and functions of like secular bodies, and whilst this is sometimes true in certain situations, its model is in fact that of the servant leadership of Christ himself, and its aim is the furtherance of the good news about him.

It is further important, then, to understand that the parish council is a council, it is not a board or an executive, and its members are not, and do not function as, directors, nor do they have executive powers.

The council is first and foremost a consultative body, called together to consult, with God and with each other, so as to discern, insofar as it is humanly possible to do so, God's will for the church in that place.

> Being a member of such a body is an extraordinary honour: In the long history of our local churches… parish council members and church leaders are entrusted with the care of the church as co-workers with God, consulting together, building on the past history of the people of God in that place, but also seeking God's will in building the future growth and development of the life of the church.[2]

The members of the parish council come together, then, to consult on matters of importance to the community they serve, seeking discernment regarding the will of God in the context of the decisions they must make, and in the discharging of those responsibilities. Its members should not be seeking to impose their will, to advance an agenda, or represent 'interest groups' within the parish, but should be constantly engaged in a process of discerning where God is leading the parish and the community they serve. Essentially, the parish council is about service, not power; its goal is missional, and it strives to be a blessing to those it serves.

Mark Tanner, in his guide for parish council members in the Church of England, sums this up well in asserting—

> A good PCC (Parochial Church Council) is a place of grace, forgiveness, prayer, wisdom and hope: it is part of Christ's body, his bride, his Church. It strives to be constructive, co-operative and cheerful. It looks up to God, looks out to the world, looks forward faithfully, and looks after others. It thinks, prays, wrestles, argues, laughs and cries, and it does it all with integrity and humility. It makes mistakes, falls short, struggles with pain, and it does all

---

2   Paul Bayes & Tim Sledge, *Mission-Shaped parish: traditional church in a changing context* (London: Church House Publishing, 2009), p. 108.

this with the same grace with which it celebrates success and the joyful moments of church life.[3]

'Grace' is a good theological word to describe the ideal operation of a parish council. All conversations, all discussions, all personal interactions and all decisions should be thoroughly grounded in, and informed by, the grace of God that is demonstrated most vividly in the life, death and resurrection of his son Jesus Christ, and ought to be reflective of the distinctly Christian character to which we are called as both individuals, and together.

> As God's chosen ones, holy and beloved, clothe yourselves with compassion, kindness, humility, meekness, and patience. Bear with one another and, if anyone has a complaint against another, forgive each other; just as the Lord has forgiven you, so you must also forgive. Above all, clothe yourself with love, which binds everything together in perfect harmony. And let the peace of Christ rule in your hearts. (Colossians 3.12–15a)

---

[3] *The PCC Member's Essential Guide: A beginners guide to hold on to!* (London: Church House Publishing, 2015), p. 8.

3. Composition of the Parish Council

The parish council includes the vicar of the parish and the churchwardens, together with a number of other laypersons who are either elected at the annual meeting or appointed by the vicar.

Qualification for membership

In order to be elected or appointed to the parish council a person must be on the electoral roll of the parish, and must be a communicant member of the Anglican Church of Australia (Rule 13.1).[4] The provisions for being included on the parish electoral roll are set out in the *Parish Governance Act 2013*, section 9. Even if on the parish electoral roll, and a communicant member, a person will be disqualified from holding office, including serving on parish council, if they are made ineligible by section 19 of the *Parish Governance Act 2013*, which prevents an undischarged bankrupt, or persons who have been convicted of a criminal offence punishable by more than five years imprisonment, or who are subject to a prohibition or order under the *Professional Standards Act*, from holding office in a parish.

Composition

The composition of the parish council is set out in the parish rules for meetings and officers, which state (Rule 10.1) that the parish council consists of—

---

[4] The Rules are located in Schedule One of the Act—see Appendix Four.

a. the vicar;
b. three churchwardens (two elected, one appointed); and
c. nine other persons, one-third (three) nominated by the vicar and two-thirds (six) elected by the parishioners.

Whilst this is the 'default,' Rule 10.1 provides for alternatives that allow the parish to have as many as 12 and as few as three in category (c).

However many parishioners are appointed and elected, the parish council, in every place, will always, in compliance with Rule 10.1, include the vicar and three churchwardens.

Upon entering the room for the first time then, the new parish council member can expect to find present the vicar of the parish (or the person who is acting as vicar if there is a vacancy) and three churchwardens, together with the members elected by the annual meeting and those appointed by the vicar.

Term of office

Apart from the vicar, and regardless of whether elected or appointed by the vicar, the term of office for each member of the parish council, including the churchwardens, is normally one year, concluding at the end of the next annual meeting (Rule 12.1). The composition of the parish council may, therefore, change at each annual meeting.

A parish may, however, adopt one of two permitted alternatives to Rule 12.2 or Rule 12.3 that provide for all, or some, of the churchwardens and/or parish council members to have overlapping two year terms.

In all cases, Rule 13.2 requires that any layperson who has been a member of the parish council for six continuous years is ineligible for election or appointment as a churchwarden, or as a member of parish council, for the next twelve months (i.e. after serving for six continuous years, a person must have a 'sabbatical' year, before being elected or appointed again).

The Vicar

The vicar is the ordained clergyperson licensed to the parish by the Archbishop, or in the event of a vacancy in the leadership of the parish, the clergyperson licensed by the Archbishop to act as the vicar (a locum). In circumstances of doubt, or if the person concerned is absent from the parish, the Archdeacon acts as the vicar. The vicar has a distinct role in the governance and management of the parish, as set out in the *Parish Governance Act 2013* section 24(c) and (d), which prescribes that the vicar—

   a. works in cooperation with the churchwardens and parish council in ensuring that the governance and management of the parish serves the identity and whole mission of the church;
   b. exercises a "presidential" role by chairing the parish council, the vestry and statutory parish meetings, or by appointing other fit persons to chair such meetings as provided for by this Act and the parish rules for meetings and officers, and is entitled to exercise a vote at a meeting of the parish council or a vestry (whether chairing the meeting or not), but is not entitled to exercise a vote at statutory parish meetings.

The vicar is always a member of the parish council in compliance with Rule 10.1a. The reality is that every community needs a leader, and, in the context of Anglican parish ministry, the vicar is that leader; like all organisations, someone needs to ensure the mechanics of communal life are in place. As John Pritchard explains, 'certain things have to be done in the life of the local church if it is to bear witness to Christ... services have to be held; people have to be cared for; Parochial Church Councils have to meet.'[5] The vicar is the person charged by the Archbishop to lead, manage and organise a parish, and to arrange the affairs of the parish, so that its mission

---

5 John Pritchard, *The life and work of a priest* (London: SPCK, 2008), p. 140.

and ministry not only happens, but is enhanced. Importantly, the vicar, as the leader of the parish, sets the culture, and bears ultimate responsibility for the good order and operation of all aspects of the parish.

The churchwardens

The churchwardens are the senior laypersons in a parish. Of the three churchwardens, two will be elected at the annual meeting (sometimes called 'peoples wardens') and one will be appointed by the vicar (sometimes referred to as the 'vicar's warden'). There is no distinction or hierarchy amongst the churchwardens. Together the churchwardens have some particular responsibilities that are set out in the *Parish Governance Act 2013*, section 23.

(1) Subject to this Act, the churchwardens of a parish are responsible for—
- a. the care and maintenance of the church, the vicarage and other accommodation provided by the parish for the staff of the parish, the church grounds, and all other buildings and property of the parish;
- b. the care of the furniture of the worship centres and of all things necessary for the conduct of public worship, and for providing everything necessary for the conduct of public worship, including the bread and wine for the Holy Communion;
- c. keeping in order the worship centres and their grounds and seeing that everything in and about the worship centres is fit and in proper order for the due performance of public worship;
- d. keeping order in the worship centres during public worship and providing for the due seating of the congregation and the collection of their offerings;
- e. reporting to the parish council all repairs or alterations

required in the fabric, fittings or furniture of the worship centres and the fabric and fittings of the vicarage;
f. complying with any laws of the Commonwealth of Australia, the State of Victoria or any municipality in which the parish has property that impose mandatory requirements applicable to the land, buildings and operations of the parish; and
g. the other functions and responsibilities imposed on them by this Act.

These are distinctive and important responsibilities that overlap with, and will require support from, the parish council, if they are to be properly discharged.

Office bearers

In addition to the vicar and churchwardens, some members of the parish council will also have particular roles and functions. Most of the provisions for such roles and functions are to be found in the parish rules for meetings and officers.

- The **Chairperson** is normally the vicar who, in the words of the *Parish Governance Act 2013*, section 24(d), 'exercises a "presidential" role by chairing the parish council.' As envisaged by that same section, however, the vicar may also appoint 'other fit persons to chair' the parish council in his or her place. Hence Rule 16, *Chairing meetings of the parish council*, states that the chair of the parish council is the vicar, but further provides for the possibility that the vicar may nominate a member of the parish council to be chair (Rule 16.1b). The chairperson occupies the most important role on the parish council, and the vicar should carefully consider whether he or she is the person best qualified to perform that role, or whether another member of the parish council is better suited to be its chairperson. Research in the business sector has shown that a very high degree of a board's effectiveness depends on the chair, who sets the agenda and determines how business is conducted.[6] In circumstances where both the vicar and a person nominated by the vicar to chair the parish council are not present at a meeting, the parish council may choose another member to be chair (Rule 16.1b). The vicar, whether chairing the meeting or not, is entitled to exercise a vote at a meeting of the parish council.

- The **Parish Treasurer** is appointed by the churchwardens (Rule 18.1), unless the parish concerned has adopted one of the permitted variations at Rule 10.1 that provide for the annual meeting to elect the treasurer, or if the parish concerned has adopted the permitted variation at Rule 18.1 which provides for the parish council to elect the treasurer. Regardless of whether appointed or elected, the treasurer must be a parishioner, and cannot also be a churchwarden without the approval of the Archbishop in Council (Rule 18.2). The treasurer is always a member of the parish council, and if not an appointed or elected member of the parish council at the time of being appointed or elected treasurer, automatically becomes one (Rule 18.3).

Rule 18.4 sets out the responsibilities of the parish treasurer as—

a. ensuring the proper banking of all moneys of the parish and the proper payment of all amounts payable by the parish;
b. maintaining proper financial records of the parish;
c. reporting to each meeting of the parish council on the financial affairs of the parish, including projected

---

6 Kevin Giles, *Making good churches better: A workbook for Church councils and Church leaders* (Melbourne: Acorn Press, 2001), p. 153.

outcomes in accordance with the annual budget of the council;

d. preparing forward estimates of income and expenditure in accordance with strategies and plans adopted by the council;

e. ensuring that the accounts of the parish are audited or assessed as required by the Act; and

f. preparing the annual financial report to the annual meeting.

- The **Parish Secretary** is always a lay member of the parish council (i.e. the parish secretary cannot be the vicar or another cleric). The parish secretary is appointed by the parish council (Rule 19.1), unless the parish concerned has adopted one of the permitted variations at Rule 10.1 which provide for the annual meeting to elect the parish secretary, or if the parish concerned has adopted the permitted variation at Rule 19.1 which provides for the churchwardens to appoint a lay member of the parish council as the parish secretary.

Rule 19.2 states that the duties of the parish secretary are determined by the parish council, however the permitted variations provide an indication of what those duties are likely to entail. They include—

a. Ensuring the minutes of parish meetings are taken and maintained;

b. Sending and receiving correspondence on behalf of the parish;

c. Maintaining an up to date compilation of the legal requirements applying to the parish;

d. Assisting the churchwardens and members of the parish council to comply with the legal requirements placed upon them.

Rule 19.2 allows for further duties to be inserted at the discretion of the parish concerned.

Others may attend

Two further categories of persons may also attend meetings of the parish council under the provisions of Rule 10.3. These are other persons in Holy Orders (i.e. ordained clergy) who are licensed to the parish, or authorised to conduct services in the parish, and lay persons appointed to stipendiary (paid) roles in the parish who are not otherwise members of the parish council. Typically these will be assistant curates or assistant priests, and authorised lay ministers leading the parish's children's ministry, youth ministry, or another form of pastoral ministry. As a matter of convention and courtesy they would normally attend at the invitation of the vicar. Parishes may further adopt alternatives to Rule 10.3 that would enable others, such as a director of music, to also attend meetings of the parish council. Anyone attending meetings of the parish council under this category (Rule 10.3) may speak at the meeting, but is not entitled to move or second motions, or vote.

It is further possible, under Rule 10.2, that the parish council may co-opt a parishioner, except for a parishioner ineligible under Rule 13, to assist the parish council in its business for a period of time; or for a person who is not a parishioner to be co-opted in the same way, as long as they are not a person ineligible under Rule 13. If the parish council does co-opt people in this way to assist it, the person attending under these provisions, as set out in Rule 10.2 and 10.4, may speak at the meeting, but is not entitled to vote.

In addition to this, and from time to time depending on the

circumstances of the parish and the business at hand, it may be desirable or necessary for members of the wider church to attend a meeting of the parish council. These may include, but are not necessarily limited to, the Area Dean, the Archdeacon, and the Bishop.

- The **Area Dean** is normally a vicar in the same geographical area (the 'deanery') who has been appointed by the Archbishop to organise meetings of the clergy in that deanery and to exercise a ministry of pastoral care to them.
- The **Archdeacon** is appointed by the Archbishop and has a particular role in the administrative, governance and missional needs of the clergy and parishes in an area, often comprising one or two deaneries. The Archdeacon is the external person most likely to appear at meetings of the parish council, especially if there is an interregnum (the time between the departure of one vicar and the appointment of the next vicar), a matter of particular strategic importance, or a difficulty of some nature.
- The **Bishop** is the senior ordained cleric with overall responsibility for the mission and ministry of a Diocese. In Melbourne, the Archbishop is the most senior cleric, and due to the size of the Diocese, is assisted by one or more Assistant Bishops.

Vacancies

A vacancy may occur if a member of the parish council resigns, ceases to be a parishioner, becomes a disqualified person under section 19 of the *Parish Governance Act 2013*, or is absent for three consecutive meetings without being granted a leave of absence, in which case their place on the parish council may be declared vacant (Rule 14.1).

A vacancy may also be created through a lack of nominees at the annual meeting.

When there is a vacancy, the position may be filled in these two ways.

1. If the vacancy is for a churchwarden or a member of the parish council appointed by the vicar, the vicar may appoint another person to fill the vacancy (Rule 15.1).
2. If the vacancy is for a churchwarden or a member of the parish council elected by an annual meeting, the whole Parish council may appoint another person to fill the vacancy.

A special election meeting is convened in the event that a vacancy causes the number of lay members of the parish council to fall to less than half its total complement of elected and appointed members (Rule 5.1).

If necessary, for instance if the person concerned was a churchwarden, the parish treasurer, or parish secretary, another member of the parish council qualified under the Act to do so may fill the vacancy and take up the role vacated (Rule 15.2).

All members are full members

Whilst some of the parish council members occupy particular roles, and whilst some, such as the churchwardens, have particular responsibilities and duties under the Act that exceed those of other members of the parish council, there ought to be no hierarchy of membership when the parish council meets and as it conducts its business. Each member of the parish council is a full member, with the same rights to speak, be heard, and contribute to decisions as any other member.

> Brother, sister let me serve you.
> Let me be as Christ to you.
> Pray that I might have the grace.
> to let you be my servant, too.
> (Richard Gillard, 1976)

4. Functions of the Parish Council

An unfortunate, but much heard, statement in the life of the church is that no one wants to be on parish council, or that being appointed or elected to a parish council is somehow a task to be endured. The stereotype is of long, boring meetings, dominated by one or two people, in which battles rage into the night over the colour of the carpet or some other inane matter. As Kevin Giles notes, in his *Making Good Churches Better*, too many members have approached the monthly council meeting with dread, anticipating a conflict-ridden talkfest that achieves little.[7] On the other hand, some vicars under-utilise the parish council at best, and at worst, see and treat it as a thing one must 'get through' rather than an opportunity for sharing mission and ministry.[8]

Even if such attitudes have their basis in an element of past truth, such a picture of the work and purpose of the parish council is a long way from the ideal and, in most places, a long way from the reality. The parish council is one of the primary ways in which those who make up the worshipping community in a particular place (the parishioners), participate with the clergy in leading and shaping the mission and ministry of God's church in that place. This is, surely, an important and weighty responsibility, to be taken seriously, and only

---

[7] *Making good churches better: A workbook for Church councils and Church leaders* (Melbourne: Acorn Press, 2001), p. 147.
[8] So David Ison (Ed), *The vicar's guide: Life and ministry in the parish* (London: Church House Publishing, 2008), p. 115.

accepted after considerable prayerful reflection and thought. Whilst matters of administration and governance, finance, property, and compliance, are a necessary part of the parish council's responsibility and must be attended to as a matter of good governance and stewardship, it is also the case that the parish council shares in the conduct of a parish's mission, and is called to focus on evangelism and outreach so that the community may grow and prosper in its proclamation of the good news about the person of Jesus Christ.

Further, it is not the case that a parish council meeting need be dull, or overly long and tedious. Much will rest on the capability of the chair, but in essence, there is no reason why a parish council need not be a place of warm engagement in mission, and its business ably executed in a timely manner, leaving room for prayer and fellowship among its members.

Functions and purpose

The *Parish Governance Act 2013*, section 25 sets out and describes the particular functions of the parish council.

1. The parish council is 'to promote the whole mission of the church, pastoral, evangelistic, social and ecumenical.' This is very broad, and includes and embraces the ministry of pastoral care and concern for others in the parish; the evangelistic ministry of the church which may encompass its outreach activities and strategies for growth; the social life of the parish; and ecumenical affairs, in particular the opportunities for working collaboratively with other Christian churches in the parish area.
2. The parish council assists the churchwardens in the discharge of their responsibilities. This is, again, a broad statement that recognises the considerable weight of responsibility the churchwardens bear. A good parish council will be constantly seeking to assist the churchwardens in their several areas

of responsibility, and looking for opportunities to share the burden with them.

3. From time to time a parish council may consider matters of particular public interest and importance concerning the Anglican Church, and might determine how to respond to them. This might arise as a result of a current matter of debate or concern in the community, especially one affecting the area in which the parish is located in some way. It should be noted that a parish council cannot make any determination or declaration regarding the doctrine, or beliefs and practices, of the Anglican Church, as any such matters, insofar as they can be changed at all, need to be considered in the context of another body such as the Synod of the diocese or the General Synod of the national church.

4. There may be occasions when the parish council may wish to raise a matter of concern or importance to it by referring that matter in some way to the Synod. The Synod may also pass legislation or motions that have an impact on the operation of the parish council, and which may require action by the parish council in order to be put into effect.

5. The parish council must, in the words of the *Parish Governance Act 2013*, 'consult together on matters of general concern and importance to the parish.' Again, this is an intentionally broad statement, that leaves open the possibility the parish council will have a significant, and wide ranging role in the affairs of the parish, especially those matters that may be of particular concern and importance to the parishioners. It is very instructive that the two key words in this clause are 'consult' and 'parish'. Consultation together, in the form of its regular meetings, and taking into consideration the views of all its members, is the essence of the life and function of the parish council. Further,

those matters of importance about which the council consult are for the whole of the parish, which in Anglican polity, implies both those who are parishioners and worshipping members of the parish church, but goes beyond this to encompass also those living in the geographical area of the parish whether they actively attend the parish church or not.

Risk management and professional standards

The parish council must have in place, and must review annually, a plan setting out the material risks and the mitigation strategies affecting the parish. This is an important matter of good governance and stewardship, noting the accountability of the parish to its community, and the imperative that the church be a place of welcome and safety for all—*Parish Governance Act 2013* section 25(3). This includes, and embraces, matters of occupational health and safety (OH&S), together with safeguarding requirements, such as police checks of all parish staff and volunteers, and ensuring those who are required to, by the nature of their roles, do have a current working with children card (WWCC).

- As leaders of the parish community, every member of parish council must themselves have both a working with children card (WWCC) and a current police check (not more than three months old at the time of appointment or election).

To fulfil its obligations in this area, the parish council should—

1. Maintain a register of the risks and hazards identified by an annual OH&S review, together with the mitigation strategies in place and corresponding action items;
2. Keep and maintain in an accessible place a list of all current policies, in particular those applying to all church workers, both paid and voluntary;
3. Keep a register of who in the parish must have a working

with children card and/or a police check, and ensure these are current for each person.

The parish council should be proactive in setting within the parish a culture of safety and compliance, and in ensuring the necessary actions are taken. It is good practice, then, that child safety, professional standards compliance, and occupational health and safety, be a standing item on the agenda.

See further: the current form of the 'Duty of Care booklet' which compiles a wealth of information, policies and procedures in the areas of child safety, professional standards, occupational health and safety, and other compliance regimes.

Finances

The *Parish Governance Act 2013*, sections 33, 34 and 35 set out the particular financial responsibilities and functions of the parish council, which include and embrace the following—

1. The parish council has general oversight, or direction, for the administration of all parish finances—*Parish Governance Act 2013*, section 33(1);
2. The parish council approves the budget for the year in which the annual meeting takes place, which it then presents to the annual meeting—*Parish Governance Act 2013*, section 33(2);
3. The parish council has power to alter the budget to respond to unforeseen, and some other, circumstances—*Parish Governance Act 2013*, section 33(4);
4. The parish council must put in place a system for monitoring how parish funds may be spent, and by whom, and how liabilities or expenses may be incurred by the parish, and by whom—*Parish Governance Act 2013*, section 34(6);
5. The parish council must ensure that certain things are paid from its funds and, in the context of its budget must

specify the amount applicable to meet these expenses. These include the supply of all things necessary for the conduct of public worship, the remuneration of parish staff, the payment of insurance premiums, the repayment of monies borrowed for building projects, and payment of the annual diocesan assessment—*Parish Governance Act 2013*, sections 33(3) and 35.

The signatories to the parish's bank account(s) are automatically the churchwardens and parish treasurer, however the parish council may appoint other signatories. The vicar must have no role in relation to the management of parish finances.

The churchwardens have additional and specific responsibilities in relation to parish finances, including ensuring receipt of the annual accounts from the parish treasurer, and ensuring that they are audited or independently examined.

Buildings and property

The parish council have some particular responsibilities in relation to the parish property and buildings, which are set out in the *Parish Governance Act 2013*, section 37—

1. The parish council must ensure that the uses of all of the parish property are consistent with the fundamental beliefs and practices of the Christian church in general, and with the good name and public reputation of the Anglican Church in particular. This may entail regulating the hire and use of the parish hall, for instance, as well as other buildings and facilities on site—*Parish Governance Act 2013*, section 37(1);
2. The parish council have a role, alongside the vicar, churchwardens and the Archbishop, in approving the altering of any existing fittings, furniture or fabric in the church, the addition

of any new fittings, furniture, or fabric, and the removal of any existing ones—*Parish Governance Act 2013*, section 37(3).

> Note: a monument or memorial cannot be fixed inside a church without a faculty being obtained from the Archbishop, and no monument or memorial for which a faculty has been previously obtained can be removed without written permission from the Archbishop—*Parish Governance Act 2013*, section 37(4–5).

Other matters

A number of other requirements are placed upon the parish council by section 25 of the *Parish Governance Act 2013*. These include, but are not limited to—

1. The parish council must take into consideration any expression of opinion by a statutory meeting of the parishioners. Typically this will be the annual meeting of parishioners, which may, for instance, resolve to ask the parish council to investigate something, or take a certain course of action—*Parish Governance Act 2013*, section 22(1);

2. The parish council must determine the amount of funds that are to be made available for the purpose of paying the parish clergy, lay ministers and other parish staff—*Parish Governance Act 2013*, section 27(1);

3. If the vicar wishes to reside beyond the geographical area of the parish boundaries, the parish council is to be consulted—*Parish Governance Act 2013*, section 38(5);

4. The time and mode of conducting the principal service of worship in a worship centre of the parish cannot be changed without the consent of both the vicar and the parish council—*Parish Governance Act 2013*, section 40(5);

5. The parish council must give written consent for a periodic

review of the parish, as set out in section 55 of the *Parish Governance Act 2013*, to be conducted—*Parish Governance Act 2013*, section 55(1);

6. The parish council is required to give written consent to any agreement for the parish to share resources, ministry, or another activity, with another parish—*Parish Governance Act 2013*, section 60(2);

7. Particular processes will apply to the parish council of a parish that is in special circumstances by virtue of being designated under the provisions of the *Parish Governance Act 2013*, section 61 as a 'supported parish', or in accordance with section 62 as a parish under 'review', or in accordance with section 72 if a parish comes 'under consideration for discontinuance'.

Evaluation

Although it is not required by the *Parish Governance Act 2013*, it may be helpful, in some instances and in some contexts, for the parish council to evaluate itself in some way. This is standard practice in many secular boards and councils, which undertake an annual stock take of the proceedings of the council, its composition, and the extent to which it is fulfilling its purposes and achieving its objectives. Various instruments may be used for this, from an open plenary session, to a simple survey, or a facilitated session with a consultant.

Shaping mission and values

The legal language in which the *Parish Governance Act 2013* is necessarily expressed gives all of this a somewhat bureaucratic, if not forensic, feel. In the midst of necessary matters such as governance, finance and the maintenance of property, it can be easy for a parish council to become bogged down in what might seem like issues of red tape and compliance, and to develop a culture that takes it away from the core business of the mission and ministry of the church. The reality is, however, that buildings, property, finance and the like are all, in themselves, missional matters too, even if they may not feel like it—for if the administrative and financial wheels of the parish are not turning as they should, its mission and ministry will soon be impeded, if not stalled. Even so, a parish council should be doing more than ensuring its particular responsibilities in corporate governance, as set out above, are being met.

The parish council has an overall responsibility for what might be summed up as the 'whole mission of the parish', as well as for shaping and influencing the values, culture and character of the parish and the people who form community in it. This is indeed a high calling, and may extend from devising, for example, in consultation with the vicar and others, a parish mission action plan (MAP), developing a parish policy for a range of matters that might include things like respectful behaviour and language, to who has access to the parish website and Facebook pages, and much more. In many places a parish will have goals or objectives, often expressed as a parish vision or mission statement, and it will be incumbent upon the parish council to monitor progress toward achieving these, and in aligning its activities with them.

It can also be useful, and at times important, to develop and make known some key, agreed statements about purpose and mission, especially where these might give rise to conflict. As Bob Jackson advises, in his highly informative and useful *Hope for the Church*, a well worded policy on a matter of contention in a parish, agreed to by the parish council, greatly assists in setting the agenda for what is and what is not important, serves to protect the vicar and others by enabling them to focus on the matters identified as mission critical, and enables all to know what the consensus view is on that issue.[9]

Because it is easy to become bogged down in small details and

---

9   Bob Jackson, *Hope for the Church: Contemporary strategies for growth* (London: Church House Publishing, 2002), p. 154.

to be delayed by matters of minor importance, and because time and resources are limited, each parish council will need to find ways of keeping mission and ministry at the forefront of their business. These might include facilitated sessions working through a resource, developing a mission action plan, or producing a parish profile and vision statement.

> Now the eleven disciples went to Galilee, to the mountain to which Jesus had directed them. When they saw him, they worshipped him; but some doubted. And Jesus came and said to them, 'All authority in heaven and on earth has been given to me. Go therefore and make disciples of all nations, baptizing them in the name of the Father and of the Son and of the Holy Spirit, and teaching them to obey everything that I have commanded you. And remember, I am with you always, to the end of the age.' (Matthew 28.16–20)

5. Communication and Representation

Although sometimes heard in the context of a discussion concerning parish council, members of a parish council should not see themselves as in some way 'representing' groups or organisations within the parish.

Despite how a person came to be a member of the parish council, and whether elected or appointed, all of the members of the parish council bear a primary responsibility under the *Parish Governance Act 2013* for the whole mission and ministry of the parish, and not for one sector, group or 'faction' within it. Deliberations and discussion, and decisions, should be taken with the best outcome for the whole of the parish in mind, with the effects and implications for individuals and groups within the parish being, of course, a valid part of the decision making. Once a decision has been taken legitimately, and with the consent of the majority present, all members of the parish council bear responsibility for it in a corporate way, and should be able to clearly and effectively communicate to the parishioners what the decision is, what it means, and the reasons for which it was taken.

Members of a parish will often, rightly and naturally, approach those who are on the parish council with a particular issue of concern or interest. Parish council members should always be open to communicating to, and with, the parishioners they represent, and should, therefore, be willing to listen respectfully to parishioners approaching them with such matters. If the matter is a difficult or divisive one, it will often be wise and necessary to refer to the vicar and/or churchwardens, or to ask the parishioner concerned to consider writing a letter setting out their question or issue of concern, addressed to the parish secretary, so that the matter can be considered as correspondence in the context of a meeting of the parish council. Individual parish council members should not normally take up, or advocate for, a particular cause or matter in the context of the meeting without giving the chair the courtesy of knowing that the matter is to be raised, especially where it may be difficult or divisive, or delay the meeting.

These words of St Paul, writing to the Romans, are as fine a summary of the marks and characteristics of Christian behaviour as ever written. Each parish council member would do well to have them firmly in mind as they come together around the table, remembering always in whose name they meet.

> Let love be genuine; hate what is evil, hold fast to what is good; love one another with mutual affection; outdo one another in showing honour. Do not lag in zeal, be ardent in spirit, serve the Lord. Rejoice in hope, be patient in suffering, persevere in prayer. Contribute to the needs of the saints; extend hospitality to strangers. Bless those who persecute you; bless and do not curse them. Rejoice with those who rejoice, weep with those who weep. Live in harmony with one another; do not be haughty, but associate with the lowly; do not claim to be wiser than you are. Do not repay anyone evil for evil, but take thought for what is noble in the sight of all. If it is possible, so far as it depends on you, live peaceably with all. (Romans 12.9–18)

6. OTHER COMMITTEES, GROUPS OR TEAMS

The *Parish Governance Act 2013* is silent on the possibility of the parish council setting up its own committees, although this is a common and often useful practice. Given their distinctive and collective responsibilities, it is to be assumed that the churchwardens will meet regularly, usually with the vicar. They do not meet as a committee of the parish council, but in order to discharge their independent statutory obligations. What committees are formed will be largely dependent on local factors, such as the size of the overall operation, past practice, and the particular needs occupying a parish council at a point in time.

The *Parish Governance Act 2013*, in section 34, provides that a person must not incur a liability on behalf of the parish except as authorised by the parish council, and that the parish council must establish a proper system for monitoring the incurring of liabilities on behalf of the parish to ensure that liabilities are incurred within the scope and terms of the authorisation given. As a result, no subcommittee, working group, or team set up by a parish council has the right to enter into any agreements with other parties on behalf of the parish without the explicit authority of the parish council. In no circumstances would that include setting up a separate bank account, or some other financial arrangement affecting the parish.

Some of the sub-committees that might be part of parish life could include, but are not limited to—

- A finance committee, although in some places the churchwardens meeting with the vicar fulfil this role;

- A worship or liturgy sub-committee, team, or working party, which shares with the vicar in planning services of worship in the parish. It should be noted, however, that the vicar has ultimate responsibility for all matters of worship and liturgy—*Parish Governance Act 2013*, section 24(a);
- Youth and/or children's and young peoples committee or planning team, to maintain the parish focus on this important aspect of its mission and ministry;
- Mission action planning (MAP) team. All parishes in the diocese are asked to have an up to date MAP in place, and many have formed a working team or planning committee to achieve this;
- Maintenance team, especially in contexts where there is a significant plant, or an ongoing need to maintain the buildings and grounds. This team is usually made up of volunteers and often led by one or more of the churchwardens;
- There may be committees for particular ministries or causes, such as supporting overseas missions and/or missionaries, outreach and evangelism, social justice issues, or for a particular matter of concern;
- There may be an ecumenical affairs team or committee made up of clergy and laypeople from neighbouring churches of different denominations, which may include representatives of the Parish council;
- In parish's where there is an opportunity shop, a school, or kindergarten, or other such enterprise, the committee of management will often comprise one or more members of the parish council, and may be constituted as a sub-committee of the parish council.

There are no requirements for a parish council to have any such sub-committees, working parties, teams, or groups, nor are there any restrictions on how many a parish council may form. As a matter of good governance it is important, however, that any committees, teams or groups formed by the parish council be given clear terms of reference, however brief, that set out the lines of accountability, and make it clear that the parish council has sole statutory responsibility for any decisions, outcomes, expenditure, and so on. which must be proposed in the form of recommendations to the parish council for resolution. It is a further matter of good governance for any committees, groups or teams formed by the parish council to be time limited, usually annually, with a view to regular review of their continued existence, terms of reference, and composition.

What then is Apollos? What is Paul? Servants through whom you came to believe, as the Lord assigned to each. I planted, Apollos watered, but God gave the growth. So neither the one who plants nor the one who waters is anything, but only God who gives the growth. The one who plants and the one who waters have a common purpose, and each will receive wages according to the labour of each. For we are God's servants, working together; you are God's field, God's building. (1 Corinthians 3.5–9)

7. Prayer

To pray is to speak to God. Throughout the scriptures we find examples of men and women spending time in prayer by speaking to God, whom we are assured, listens to and receives our prayers. It will be natural then, for a parish council to begin in prayer, and indeed, every meeting of every parish council should. In some parishes the parish council meeting may be preceded by a service of Holy Communion, Evening Prayer, or a prayer meeting, or may begin with a reading and devotion from the Bible that leads into the opening prayers. In other places, the vicar may lead prayers, or members of the parish council may take it in turns to lead the prayers.

A Prayer Book for Australia 1995 includes a prayer for use 'Before a Meeting' (p. 213).

God our Creator,
When you speak there is light and life
Fill us with your Holy Spirit
So that we may listen to one another,
Speak the truth in love,
and bear much fruit in the service of your kingdom,
through Jesus Christ our Lord. Amen.

A Prayer Book for Australia contains further prayers for 'Various Occasions' and several 'Thanksgivings' (pp. 183–222) that may be suitable for use in a range of circumstances – from longer litanies, to prayers for choosing a new incumbent, to those for use in times of international conflict or disaster, as well as prayers of intercession for the church, discipleship and mission. Of course, the Lord's Prayer may also be used, said by all, as a way of gathering up the prayers, both spoken and silent, of all present.

Many parish councils will conclude with the members standing to say together 'The Grace', a benediction (closing prayer or blessing) taken from the end of St Paul's second letter to the Corinthians.

The grace of the Lord Jesus Christ,

And the love of God

And the fellowship of the Holy Spirit,

Be with us all evermore. Amen.

Mark Tanner, in his *The PCC Member's Essential Guide*, makes three further, excellent suggestions, regarding prayer.[10]

1. **Prayer Walks.** Print out a map of the parish area and plot several routes through it, walking through each over time, praying for the things you observe along the way. This can be done alone, or in groups, over an extended period of time.

2. **Praying the papers.** Obtain the local paper each week and take time to carefully and prayerfully read it, noting the major issues affecting the local area and praying for them, and for those involved in, and impacted by, them.

3. **The prayer box.** Sometimes people can be reticent to pray aloud, or may find it difficult to respond immediately when asked to provide prayer requests. A prayer box, placed in the back of the church or where people fellowship together after the service, can be used to collect prayer requests on scraps of paper, that parish council can use to guide their prayers.

There are many other ways a parish council may engage in prayer, and ensure it spends time seeking God, and talking to God.

Rejoice always, pray without ceasing, give thanks in all circumstances; for this is the will of God in Christ Jesus for you. (1 Thessalonians 5.16–18).

See: Appendix Two for Prayers for use by parish councils.

---

10 *The PCC Member's Essential Guide: A beginners guide to hold on to!* (London: Church House Publishing, 2015), pp. 34-35.

8. Consulting Together

As we have seen, a primary purpose and function of the parish council is to 'consult together on matters of general concern and importance to the parish.' This entails meetings, and for many, probably most, members of the parish council, attending meetings of the parish council will be their primary point of involvement.

The parish council is required to 'hold such meetings as are necessary for the performance of its functions' (Rule 22.1). Some parishes may wish to set a minimum number of meetings, or set a regular occurrence (e.g. monthly), by adopting one of the two permitted variations to Rule 22.1. Most parish councils will have an established pattern of meeting, often monthly (e.g. the first Tuesday evening in each month, except January), but some will set the meeting pattern and frequency at the first meeting of the new parish council following the annual meeting, so that the pattern is agreed to by the majority of the members. The most common pattern is monthly meetings (usually except January), with most parish councils meeting in the evening, although some meet on the weekend. Many parish councils also have an annual or bi-annual planning day, often at the start of the year, and some have a weekend away or retreat.

In addition to the regular meetings, as established by the parish council, there are provisions for further extraordinary meetings, should such meetings be required or become necessary.

1. The vicar, or the chair if a person other than the vicar, can convene a meeting at any time, subject to any direction made by the parish council concerned (Rule 22.2).

2. A meeting of the parish council can be convened upon the request of four members (Rule 22.3).

The quorum, apologies and leave of absence

For a meeting to proceed, whether a regular scheduled meeting or an extraordinary one called according to the provisions above, there must be a quorum of members present. The quorum set by the *Parish Governance Act 2013* (Rule 11.1) is a simple majority (i.e. more than half of the total number of members), although this can be altered to a greater proportion if the permitted variation is adopted.

If a member of the parish council is unable to be present at a meeting, they should advise the chair or the parish secretary of their inability to attend, and should ask to be noted as an apology in the minutes of the meeting. There is no provision for voting by proxy (i.e. having a person who is present vote on another member's behalf).

If a member of parish council is aware they will not be able to be present for more than two consecutive meetings, they should request a leave of absence for the number of meetings they expect to miss, and ask that this be recorded in the minutes. A leave of absence might be necessary in instances of extended travel, or during a period of illness or hospitalisation, for example. Where leave of absence is granted, or when it is known that a member of parish council is unable to fulfil their duties for a period of time, an 'acting appointment' may be made by following the provisions of Rule 21.1.

Voting

There will be occasions at most meetings of the parish council when a vote is called for. Often this will be routine—for example, the minutes of each meeting are normally ratified at the next meeting, after a call for alterations, corrections, or additions, and are then formally approved as a true and accurate record by a vote of the members present. Similarly, the correspondence to be tabled and dealt with, and the reports, including the financial statements, will be ratified by a vote of all present.

The procedure for this is that a member 'moves' a motion, for example, that the minutes be approved, or that the correspondence or a particular report be received. The mover is often the person presenting the report. Another member of the parish council must second this for it to then become a 'motion'. A motion may be amended, and, following any discussion, is then put to the vote, usually by show of hands but sometimes by voices ('aye' or 'no'). In some especially contentious or difficult circumstances the vote may be by secret ballot. If the vote on a motion is even (i.e. six for and six against), the motion is resolved in the negative (it is lost—Rule 22.4). Whilst the chair of the parish council has a vote, as does every member of the parish council, neither the vicar not the person chairing the meeting (if the vicar is not the chair) has a 'casting vote' in the event there is an even number of votes on a matter under consideration (Rule 22.5).

Matters for which there is a motion, and, consequently, which are to be resolved by a vote of the members of the parish council, will normally be clearly indicated on the agenda that is distributed in advance of the meeting. This is good governance, and the chair of the parish council should make the usual procedures for decision making and voting known to the members at the first meeting of a new parish council, or in some other way. It is possible, however, for any member of the parish council to move a motion during the course of a meeting, whether it has been advised in advance of the meeting or not. If seconded, the motion must then be dealt with in the way outlined above.

In addition to receiving the minutes, correspondence and reports, any item of business that requires the expenditure of parish funds should be expressed as a motion, be moved and seconded, and then put to the vote, in the manner described above. This is because an auditor or independent examiner will look through the minutes of the parish council to ensure that expenditure, and especially any un-budgeted expenses, were agreed to. In addition, if such a motion represents a departure from the parish's budget, there should be a separate motion duly considered and passed to amend the budget. From time to time, there may be other motions put before the parish council in a formal way – often these will be accompanied by a presentation, written report, or speech supporting the motion, and discussed at the parish council meeting ahead of the motion being put to the vote.

Conflicts of interest

It is important to note that a member of the parish council cannot vote on a matter in which he or she has a conflict of interest, and should normally leave the meeting when that matter is reached on the agenda to avoid being present for both the discussion and any vote resulting. By 'conflict of interest' is meant a matter in which a person has a pecuniary interest (Rule 23.1). This will normally be a matter in which the person concerned, or another person with whom they are associated, has a reasonable likelihood or expectation of gaining or benefiting in some way. An example of this will be a motion to award a contract for roofing repairs on the parish vicarage to a company owned by the spouse or partner of a member of the parish council. Another example would be where the son or daughter of a parish council member is on the committee of a community service organisation that wanted to hire the hall for meetings. At the time this matter comes up for discussion on the agenda at a meeting of the parish council, the person concerned must declare a conflict of interest, and offer to leave the meeting until the matter is resolved and the next item on the agenda is reached (Rules 23.1–3).

The minutes

The *Parish Governance Act 2013* (Rule 22.6) requires that 'true and accurate records of each meeting of the parish council shall be kept and signed by the chair.' Normally, the parish secretary will take and keep the minutes, which are then distributed after the meeting to all members of the parish council, and ratified at the following meeting. The chair will then sign a copy of the minutes as agreed upon, after any corrections, alterations or additions requested by the meeting have been made. The *Parish Governance Act 2013* further requires that the minutes of the parish council are 'publicly displayed' (Rule 24.1). A permitted variation to this rule, however, allows a parish council to alter this provision by specifying how the minutes are publicly displayed (e.g. on the parish website), whilst a further permitted variation leaves open the possibility of this requirement being omitted altogether.

Relationship and community

At its heart, the parish council, like the parish itself, is a community, made up of people called out of the broader community of the parish for a season of time to assist with the governance and leadership of that parish in the context of the parish council. The council is, then, a network of interpersonal relationships. At its best, it should be a reflection of the diversity of the parish, and it should take the lead in modelling and reflecting Christian community to the parish. As Paul Bayes & Tim Sledge note,[11] a good question a parish council might ask itself is, are we truly a body, in the way that St Paul describes a body of believers in his first letter to the Corinthians?

> For just as the body is one and has many members, and all the members of the body, though many, are one body, so it is with

---

11 *Mission-Shaped parish: traditional church in a changing context* (London: Church House Publishing, 2009), p. 110.

Christ. For in the one Spirit we were all baptized into one body—Jews or Greeks, slaves or free—and we were all made to drink of one Spirit. Indeed, the body does not consist of one member but of many. (1 Corinthians 12.12-14)

9. Preparing for the Meeting

In order to participate fully in the discussion and decision-making that typically takes place at a meeting of the parish council, it is important that council members spend some time in preparation for the meeting. This need not be especially onerous or time consuming, unless perhaps if there is a matter of particular importance, controversy, or difficulty on the agenda.

Some simple things that can be done to prepare for a meeting are—

- Ensure the dates and times of each meeting are safely in your schedule for the whole year ahead. If you cannot attend a meeting, advise the chair or parish secretary that you will be an **apology** in advance of the meeting. Although it is not possible for a proxy to attend in your place and speak or vote on your behalf, most chairs will allow you to provide some written notes on any item on the agenda for which you may wish your views to be made known to the meeting.
- **Read** the papers distributed in advance of the meeting. The discussion is likely to be conducted on the assumption that members of the parish council have read the content of the reports and other papers provided to them in advance of the meeting, and have come prepared to consider and discuss.
- **Communication** is an essential part of the smooth running of any committee or organisation. Ensure you read and respond to messages from the chair, parish secretary, or other members of the parish council, in a timely manner. It is likely much

communication among the members of the council will be by email, and there may well be email updates on matters raised, or to be raised, at parish council meetings.
- **Engage** with the parishioners and other stakeholders as appropriate on the matters being discussed and deliberated by the parish council. It is always good and helpful for parish council members to be aware of the thoughts and views of the parishioners.
- Whilst noting the need for good communication, and for engagement with parishioners and other stakeholders, members of parish council will also recognise and observe **confidentiality** where appropriate and as instructed by the chair.
- Finally, the parish council is, of course, an important part of a Christian community, and as Christians, its members should always be immersed in **prayer**. Pray for the workings of the parish council, for the matters to be discussed and decided upon, for the other members of the council, and for the work and mission of God's Church.

Whilst everyone will prepare in their own way, it can be helpful to make notes as you read through the papers, underlining things of importance and identifying matters about which you may wish to ask questions. If there are long and complex papers, it can sometimes help to read the summary at the beginning and end first, so as to gain an overall understanding of the matter. Similarly, the financial statements can sometimes appear like a wall of numbers, but often there will be some commentary in writing to accompany them, explaining the figures, and setting out the assumptions that underlie them.

The 'Prayer of Preparation' (*A Prayer Book for Australia* 1995)
Almighty God,
to whom all hearts are open,
all desires known,

and from whom no secrets are hidden:
cleanse the thoughts of our hearts
by the inspiration of your Holy Spirit,
that we may perfectly love you,
and worthily magnify your holy name,
through Christ our Lord. Amen.

10. What Happens at a Parish Council Meeting?

Although it is hard to be specific, given the great variety of parishes and the communities they serve across the Diocese of Melbourne, and because much will depend on the chair who sets the direction for the meeting and prepares and sets the agenda; there are some things that will be relatively universal and common to most parish council meetings. Each meeting of the parish council will have been prepared in advance, and in most cases, an agenda, together with the minutes of the previous meeting, reports such as the vicar's report, and the financial statements, will be sent to the members prior to the meeting.

The agenda

The meeting will follow a format set by the agenda, which outlines what will happen in sequential order. There are some things that will appear on the agenda of every regular meeting. The agenda helps organise and guide the meeting, ensuring that matters of importance are not missed, and will usually advise of any motions for decision. The agenda might identify the person responsible for presenting a particular matter, for example, the vicar's report (the vicar) or the financial statements (the treasurer). A time frame (e.g. 15 mins, or 6.00–6.15pm) may also be allocated to each item, to help guide the meeting (and the chair).

A typical agenda may include the following—

1. **Identification of the date and time of the meeting, and the venue:** in addition to a starting time, the agenda may also indicate a finishing time, so that the meeting is kept within a defined, and agreed to, period of time.
2. **Welcome:** the chair welcomes those present to the meeting.
3. **Prayers:** most meetings will commence in prayer.
4. **Apologies:** any apologies or requests for leave of absence, which should have been communicated to the chair in advance of the meeting, will be noted.
5. **Notice of any conflicts of interest:** may be called for as the meeting commences, or alternatively, the practice may be that conflicts of interest be declared as they arise throughout the meeting.
6. **Minutes of the previous meeting:** the minutes of the previous meeting will normally have been distributed in advance for members to read and check, ahead of them being ratified, with any alterations or corrections, at the meeting.
7. **Matters arising from the minutes of the previous meeting:** a matter arising is something that is present in the previous meeting's minutes, which is not otherwise covered by the agenda, but may require further discussion and/or resolution.
8. **Child safety, professional standards compliance, and OH&S** (recommended to be a standing item on the agenda).
9. **Correspondence:** any items of correspondence, that have been received by post, email or other means, are tabled as 'correspondence in'; whilst any correspondence that the parish secretary, or another member of the parish council, has sent in the name of the parish council since the last meeting is noted as 'correspondence out'. The correspondence (in and out) may be 'received' by the moving of a motion to do so.
10. **Reports:** There may be written or verbal reports from a

variety of people. Normally the vicar will provide a report. Often the churchwardens will also report on any matters for which they have carriage. There may be reports from other ministers and areas of ministry, including the Sunday School, youth ministry, choir, Mothers Union, and so on. For some parishes it may be helpful to receive these reports quarterly and consider them by rotation at different meetings. It is possible that the content of the reports may lead to a resolution being moved to take a certain course of action, which will need to be ratified by a vote.

11. **Finances:** the financial statements will normally be tabled at each meeting of the parish council by the parish treasurer, who will often summarise them and take relevant questions. The financial statements are received by the meeting through the putting of a motion (normally by the treasurer) to adopt them, which is then seconded by another member of the parish council, and a vote taken.

12. **General business:** this is the opportunity to raise any matters for discussion and deliberation that are not covered elsewhere on the agenda, or for which there is not a natural place on the agenda for them to be raised. It is customary, and a matter of good governance, that the chair be advised in advance of the meeting, or sometimes at the beginning of the meeting, of an intention to raise matters of general business.

13. **Close:** the meeting will be declared closed and the time noted. Many parish councils will end with a short prayer said by all, such as 'The Grace'.

14. **The date and time, and venue, of the next meeting:** this will normally be noted at the end of the agenda.

Each agenda will look different, depending on local custom, and some may be more formal than others, but most will include at least some of the features identified above.

During the meeting

Each member of the parish council may ask questions, especially where something is unclear or unknown to them. There is no such thing as 'a stupid question'. In most cases, the person responsible for answering will be pleased and able to do so immediately, or will undertake to provide an answer at the next meeting or at another convenient time. It is possible, if not probable, that other members of the parish council might have wondered about the same thing, but have been reticent to ask. Asking questions is a matter of good governance.

On some occasions, for example, if there are many questions to ask, or a significant amount of detail that will need to be provided, it may be best to seek a meeting with the responsible person outside of the Parish council meeting, so that the meeting is not delayed or dominated by a matter that not all members will be interested in pursuing. For instance, a member of the parish council may have a number of questions about the financial reports that might not be of high importance or interest to other members of the parish council, and in those circumstances might ask to meet with the parish treasurer at another time to look over the accounts and ask questions about them.

Each member of a parish council should feel free to participate in the discussion on any matter under consideration at the meeting, especially if they feel they may have something to contribute to it. Sometimes this will take the form of asking a question, sometimes it will be adding some knowledge or insight to a matter under discussion, and at other times it will be forming a view and participating in the debate. It is not the case, however, that every member of the parish council need, or should, have something to say about every matter on the agenda, at every meeting.

Fellowship

Because the parish council is a community, and because the strength, or otherwise, of a community relies on the quality of the relationships within it, adequate time should always be set aside, in the context of a Parish council, for fellowship. Most typically this will take place after the meeting, over a cup of coffee or tea, or a glass of wine, and often accompanied by supper. Some councils produce a roster for this purpose. Whilst the conclusion of the meeting is a natural place for fellowship, it is not the only possibility, and may not always be the most ideal, especially if members need to return home quickly after a long day at work, or if the meeting has run overtime. Some parish councils may offer a time of fellowship before the meeting begins, and some have a regular or annual meal, at which partners of members are also often invited. Depending on the manner in which the meeting is chaired, and taking care to stick to the agenda, it is also possible for there to be an adjournment in the middle of the meeting for a short break and fellowship.

After the meeting

Kevin Giles writes that, in his experience, one of the most significant faults of a church council is the failure of its members to take responsibility for the council's decisions.

> Most people like being on church council, enjoy the talking, love being at the centre of the decision-making process but fail to do the follow up work required. This means that motions are passed but action does not follow.[12]

This is a corporate responsibility, and also a function of the chair, who should clearly note who is responsible for ensuring a course of action is carried out to completion, upon the successful passing of

---

12 *Making good churches better: A workbook for Church councils and Church leaders* (Melbourne: Acorn Press, 2001), p. 156.

a motion or a resolution to do so. Some parish councils will keep an 'action tracker' to help them keep track of who is undertaking a certain task, and all should, at the very least, record in the minutes how a motion, or another expression of the council's will, is to be expedited, by whom, and within what time frame.

If you have been asked to perform some task or action and have agreed to do so, ensure you make a note of it, and do it. Much of the business of the parish council will be carried out after the meeting, and its effectiveness, or otherwise, will depend on its members being proactive in carrying out things they have agreed to do or participate in. It can also be wise, and helpful, to open a file, either a physical or digital one, or both, in which meeting notes, the agenda, reports and minutes, together with anything you might be directly responsible for or have undertaken to bring through to fruition, can be kept, and referred to after the meeting, as may be necessary.

> The Church's councils can act as microcosm of the Church as it should be. They can adopt a lifestyle which is open, honest and rooted in God and committed to seeking the advancement of the kingdom. If they do, then the structures of the Church can and do work well for mission.[13]

---

13 Paul Bayes & Tim Sledge, *Mission-Shaped parish: traditional church in a changing context* (London: Church House Publishing, 2009), p. 121.

11. The Annual Meeting

The annual meeting is an opportunity for all of the parishioners to gather together and to hear about the life and work of the parish, reflect on the past year, and consider the future. As we have seen, the members of the parish council are elected at this meeting – if there are to be elections. The parish rules for meetings and officers sets out the process for calling and conducting the annual Meeting, together with how the parish council is elected and appointed.

The electoral roll

Each parish maintains an electoral roll containing the names of those laypersons aged over eighteen who have met the qualification for being on the parish electoral roll, and have filled out and signed an application form. The qualifications and procedure for this is to be found in the *Parish Governance Act 2013* section 9. In short, to be on the electoral roll, a person must—

- Be a layperson (i.e. not ordained);
- Be over eighteen years of age;
- Be baptised;
- Have regularly and habitually attended public worship in that parish;
- Be a member of the Anglican Church of Australia;
- Not be a member of another church or denomination;
- Not be on the electoral roll of another parish or congregation;
- Have completed and signed an application to be on the electoral roll.

The electoral roll is maintained by the parish electoral committee, as set out in the *Parish Governance Act 2013*, section 10, which requires—

> There to be a parish electoral committee; comprising the vicar and either a churchwarden or a member of the parish council; appointed by the parish council at its first meeting after the annual meeting.
>
> The parish electoral committee has the task of maintaining and revising the parish electoral roll each year, in advance of the annual meeting, in accordance with the provisions of the *Parish Governance Act 2013*, sections 11 and 12.
>
> **Note:** it is up to each parish electoral committee to determine whether a person has regularly and habitually attended public worship in the parish, and it is anticipated that appropriate pastoral sensitivity and common sense will be applied, especially where, for example, a member of a parish may have to travel interstate or overseas for work. Under the provisions of the Parish Governance Act a person who has attended public worship at a worship centre 12 times in the preceding 12 months and three times in the preceding three months is deemed to have regularly and habitually attended public worship.

Statutory meetings

A statutory meeting means any meeting called under the provisions of the *Parish Governance Act 2013*. This may be a meeting called for a special purpose, an extraordinary meeting of the parishioners on the electoral roll, or for the purposes of conducting an election, deciding on a change to worship times or style, to decide on a co-operation with a neighbouring parish, or whether to place the parish under consideration. There is, however, only one statutory meeting that must take place every year, and that is the annual meeting. For most parishes, in most years, the annual meeting will be the only statutory meeting held in the parish.

The financial year

The financial year followed by the church is different to the financial year of the secular world (1 July – 30 June), and distinct to the calendar year as reckoned by secular time. In the church, a new financial and administrative year begins annually on 1 October. This means that the end of the financial year in the church is 30 September (*Parish Governance Act 2013* section 3). The 1 October date has several implications—

- The financial statements will close on 30 September, and will then need to be audited or independently examined, with the audit or examination being concluded in time for the annual accounts to be presented to the annual Meeting;
- The budget set by the parish council, and presented to the annual Meeting, will commence each year on 1 October (i.e. not from the date of the annual meeting or from 1 January or another date);
- The parish records, such as the average number attending services of worship, and the number of baptisms, weddings and funerals are calculated for the period 1 October to 30 September;
- A new stipend determination, setting out the rates at which the clergy and any authorised stipendiary lay ministers are remunerated (paid), will take effect on 1 October each year, and will need to be signed by the churchwardens and the cleric or lay minister concerned before that date.

Annual meeting 'season'

The annual meeting of the parish must be held in either October or November each year (Rule 3.1). Several things must be done in advance of the annual Meeting, including, but not limited to—

- The fixing of the time and date of the annual meeting, by the parish council;

- The preparation of the agenda;
- The preparation of reports by those responsible, and the collation of the reports;
- The auditing, or independent examination, of the accounts;
- The revision of the parish electoral roll by the parish electoral committee;
- The call for nominations for churchwarden, parish council, and incumbency committee.

This activity gives the month or so leading up to the Annual meeting the feel of a season of its own, often referred to as 'annual meeting season'. In addition to this, the annual meeting of the Synod of the diocese will be held during the course of the month of October. Synod is modelled on parliament, and will extend for three sessions over the course of three years, and is attended by the licensed clergy of the diocese and the lay representatives elected every three years by each parish in the diocese.

The annual meeting

The manner of calling and conducting the annual meeting is set out in schedule one of the *Parish Governance Act 2013* which contains the 'parish rules for meetings and officers'. In addition to fixing the time and date of the meeting, the parish council must issue a notice giving parishioners advice of the arrangements for the annual meeting together with details of the time and date by which nominations are to be received (Rule 3.2). All nominations, for all positions, are to be displayed at the entrance to the main place of worship for at least 48 hours before the commencement of the annual meeting (Rule 3.3).

Rule 3.4 sets out the order of business that must be part of the annual meeting, although there may be additional business—
- Prayers;
- The minutes of the previous annual meeting;

- Reception of the electoral roll;
- An annual report by the vicar;
- An annual report on the proceedings of the parish council;
- An annual report by the churchwardens;
- The audited, or independently examined, accounts;
- The budget approved by the parish council for the year in which the annual meeting takes place;
- Reports by other parish groups;
- The election of churchwardens and members of the parish council;
- The election of representatives to the parish incumbency committee;
- The election of the parish incumbency committee reserve list (if desired);
- The election of an auditor or independent examiner;
- Any other matters of parochial or general church interest.

The vicar chairs the annual meeting but does not have a vote and does not, therefore, have a casting vote (Rules 7.1 and 7.2). The quorum is that set by Rule 7.3—either one-fifth of those on the electoral roll or ten parishioners, whichever is the greater.

> **Note:** if the written report of the auditor or independent examiner has not been distributed to those present at the annual meeting, the meeting must be adjourned (when all other business has been dealt with) to a later date (but before the end of February) so that the report can be seen and received.

Elections

As noted earlier, the parish council is composed of those elected by the annual meeting of the parishioners, and those appointed by the vicar, in the proportions determined by Rule 10.1. At the time the annual meeting is called there is also a call for nominations for churchwarden, members of the parish council, members of the incumbency committee, and members of the incumbency committee reserve list (Rule 8.1). There are no nominations for, and there is no election at the annual meeting of, Synod representatives. The Synod representatives are elected every three years upon receipt of the Archbishop's mandate for the calling of a new Synod.

The procedure for elections is set out in Rule 9—
- If at the time the nominations close, the number of nominees is equal to, or less than, the number of vacancies, all nominated will be elected unopposed;
- If there are fewer nominees than positions available, there will be a casual vacancy that may be filled under the provisions of Rule 15;
- If an election is required, it is conducted by secret ballot and overseen by a returning officer appointed by the vicar;
- If there is an equality of votes requiring a casting vote, the returning officer has the casting vote, or may decide by the casting of lots.

The churchwardens and members of the parish council elected at the annual meeting will normally hold office until the conclusion of the next annual meeting, unless the parish concerned has adopted a permitted variation for two-year terms.

Appointments

The vicar appoints one of the three churchwardens, the other two being elected by the annual meeting (Rule 17.1). In all of the possible compositions set out under Rule 10.1, the parish council will be composed of a proportion of those elected by the annual meeting and a lesser proportion appointed by the vicar (Rule 12.1).

The vicar is required to announce to the parishioners the name of the person appointed as churchwarden, and the names of those appointed as members of the parish council, within 30 days of the annual meeting (Rule 20.1).

The churchwardens and members of the parish council appointed by the vicar, as with those elected by the annual meeting, will hold office until the conclusion of the next annual meeting (Rule 12.1), unless one of the permitted variations allowing for two years terms has been adopted.

After the annual meeting

It is just as important that the vicar, churchwardens and parish secretary (especially) do not lose sight of the important reporting requirements that follow the annual meeting. In fact, it is wise to think of the annual meeting as not truly ending until all the subsequent actions have been completed. These include—

- Having appropriate police checks and/or working with children cards sought and obtained;
- Having new parish council members sign the required declarations (see the Parish Governance Regulations—Appendix Four);
- Appointing the churchwarden who is to be the wardens' appointee on the incumbency committee;
- Notifying the registrar of the members of the incumbency committee;
- Within seven days of the conclusion of the annual meeting send to the registrar two copies of the accounts and financial documents prepared for the meeting.

Many parishes also include a commissioning of those newly elected during one or more of the Sunday services following the annual meeting or early in the new year.

In the year that King Uzziah died, I saw the Lord sitting on a throne, high and lofty; and the hem of his robe filled the temple.

Seraphs were in attendance above him; each had six wings: with two they covered their faces, and with two they covered their feet, and with two they flew. And one called to another and said: 'Holy, holy, holy is the Lord of hosts; the whole earth is full of his glory.' The pivots on the thresholds shook at the voices of those who called, and the house filled with smoke. And I said: 'Woe is me! I am lost, for I am a man of unclean lips, and I live among a people of unclean lips; yet my eyes have seen the King, the Lord of hosts!' Then one of the seraphs flew to me, holding a live coal that had been taken from the altar with a pair of tongs. The seraph touched my mouth with it and said: 'Now that this has touched your lips, your guilt has departed and your sin is blotted out.' Then I heard the voice of the Lord saying, 'Whom shall I send, and who will go for us?' And I said, 'Here am I; send me!' (Isaiah 6.1–8)

12. Through the Year

The church year has a rhythm that distinguishes it from the calendar year. Hence theologians talk about the marking of 'liturgical time' or 'sacred time', separate to that of secular time. Sacred time is marked by the seasons of the church year, but also by the routines and rhythms of the annual meeting and the business of the parish council, which provide a place and an opportunity for parishioners to become involved in the administrative, governance and financial life of their parish, as well as its worshipping life.

Advent

The church year begins at Advent, which will commence either late in November or early in December. The season of Advent occupies the four weeks prior to Christmas, and is a period of preparation for the annual celebration of the birth of our Lord. As Advent is a time of preparation, violet or purple is the liturgical colour. The commencement of the church year on Advent Sunday, the Sunday that commences the season of Advent, often has a symmetry with the commencement of a new parish council, following the annual meeting, which must be held in October or November.

Christmas and Epiphany

Whilst it has become commonplace to think of and to speak about the season of Christmas as the period of time leading up to 25 December each year, the reckoning of liturgical or sacred time finds otherwise. The season of Christmas begins on Christmas Eve and extends to the Feast of the Epiphany (marking the visit of the Magi to the infant Jesus) on

6 January. As a celebratory festival, the liturgical colour for Christmas is white. After the Epiphany, the church enters a period of 'ordinary time', during which the Sundays that fall between Epiphany and the beginning of Lent on Ash Wednesday will be called the Sundays after Epiphany (or Epiphany 1, Epiphany 2, and so on). During 'ordinary time' green is the liturgical colour. In Australia, the Epiphany itself, and the first few weeks afterwards, will coincide with the holiday month of January for many people. Many parish councils will not meet during January, although some may have a planning session, sometimes over a whole day, or even a whole weekend, early in the new year.

Lent

The season of Lent begins on Ash Wednesday, and marks the forty days (not counting the Sundays) before the commencement of Holy Week and Easter. Lent is a penitential season, in preparation for Easter, during which time Christians are called to prayer, reflection and self-examination. As a season of preparation, the liturgical colour during Lent is the same as Advent—violet or purple.

Holy Week and Easter

The most important week in the church's year commences with Palm, or Passion, Sunday and ends with Easter Day. The week concludes with the three great days, often called the 'Easter Triduum,' Maundy Thursday, recalling the Last Supper; Good Friday, remembering the crucifixion of Jesus; and Holy Saturday, the day between Good Friday and Easter Day. These are the last few days of the season of Lent, which will conclude with the celebration of the Lord's resurrection on Easter Day.

Easter

Although often compressed into a single day or weekend by the weight of secular time, in the Church, the season of Easter extends for several weeks, commencing with the celebration of the resurrection of Jesus on Easter Day, and extending to the Day of Pentecost.

Pentecost

The Day of Pentecost falls 50 days after Easter, and celebrates the coming of the Holy Spirit and the beginning of the Christian church, as described in chapter 2 of the Acts of the Apostles. Red is worn on the Day of Pentecost, for the 'tongues of fire' that descended on those gathered in the upper room. The Sunday after Pentecost is Trinity Sunday. After this, a long period of 'ordinary time' commences, during which the Sundays will be designated 'after Pentecost' (or Pentecost 1, Pentecost 2, and so on). As a period of ordinary time, the liturgical colour is green.

All Saints and Remembrance

The church year, or liturgical year, which began on Advent Sunday, draws to its conclusion in the month of November, which begins with the observance of All Saints Day on 1 November. As a festival, or celebration, the liturgical colour for All Saints is white. In many places All Souls Day on 2 November may also be observed, whilst there might also be a service for Remembrance Day on 11 November. The church year will come to an end during the month of November on the Sunday prior to Advent Sunday, which is celebrated as Christ the King Sunday.

Other occasions

In addition to the marking of sacred time and the annual rhythm of the seasons of the church year, many, if not most, parishes will mark other important occasions throughout the course of the year. Many will be well-established annual events in the life of the parish community, while others may be one off or exceptional occasions. The parish council may well have a significant role to play in the planning and execution of these special days, which may include, but will not be limited to the following.

- Ordinations: Although ordinations will normally take place at the Cathedral, if the parish has a new assistant curate these occasions will be important ones in the church year. Most deacons are ordained in early February, and priests in late November.
- Episcopal visits: The Archbishop, or a bishop, may visit during the course of the year, for an important festival, an anniversary, or just to preside and preach in the parish.
- If there is a Confirmation, a bishop will visit to conduct the service.
- The patronal festival may be a significant event in the life of the parish. The patronal festival is named after the 'patron' saint, or the 'holy mystery,' for which the church is named. For instance, if St Mary's, the patronal festival will be on 15 August (or the Sunday nearest) which is the Feast Day of Mary, Mother of our Lord; or if Holy Trinity, then the patronal festival will be on Trinity Sunday, and so on.
- The parish fete, fair or community open day, if a custom, or another comparable event, may be a particular focus at a certain time of year.

Lord, for the years your love has kept and guided,
urged and inspired us, cheered us on our way,
sought us and saved us, pardoned and provided:
Lord for the years, we bring our thanks today.
(Timothy Dudley-Smith, 1969)

13. When the Vicar Leaves

A range of things occurs when a vicar leaves a parish. Because a parish is a community, it is natural that strong relationships of mutual trust and Christian fellowship may develop between the parishioners and the leader of the community. When the leader moves on, there will often be a degree of sadness and a sense of loss, before acceptance of the new situation sets in, and the need to appoint a successor becomes the primary consideration.

At the time the vicar formally leaves, or sometimes before the nominal date if there are periods of annual leave or long service leave pending, the bishop responsible will appoint a locum, to ensure that pastoral and sacramental ministry will continue. Any other members of the parish staff, such as assistant curates, assistant or honorary priests, and authorised lay ministers, will continue in their roles, as will the churchwardens and the parish council. It is important to note that the locum minister who is appointed has all of the rights, privileges and responsibilities of the vicar. So the *Parish Governance Act 2013* section 3 (in the definitions) advises that, where there is a locum appointed to the parish, that person is regarded as the vicar for the purposes of the Act.

The churchwardens and parish council, and of course the incumbency committee representatives, will have some extra tasks and duties to perform during the period of an interregnum (the period of time until the new vicar arrives) and whilst a locum is in place. In most instances, the locum will be a retired priest working part time, and so there will be aspects of the life of the church that others will need to pick up in the absence of a full-time vicar. A significant task needing to be undertaken, that will often become the responsibility of the parish council, is the preparation of a parish profile, which will be used to give prospective vicars a sense of the parish situation and its ministry. This entails setting out in a document the main ministries of the parish, including its Sunday services, and taking stock of the numbers attending, the buildings and property, and the finances, together with the mission action plan and its implementation and progress.

The parish council will play a key role in ensuring the parish continues to function during the period of waiting for a new vicar, and may be well served by ensuring frequent use among the parishioners, and in communal contexts such as Sunday services and meetings of the parish council, of the prayer below, for use at the time of choosing an incumbent, from *A Prayer Book for Australia 1995*.

Bountiful God,
give to this parish a faithful pastor
who will faithfully speak your word
and minister your sacraments;
an encourager who will equip your people for ministry
and enable us to fulfil our calling.
Give to those who will choose, wisdom,
discernment and patience,
and to us give warm and generous hearts,
for Jesus Christ's sake. Amen.

Appendix One
Glossary

***A Prayer Book for Australia* 1995 (*APBA*):** the authorised liturgy for use in the Anglican Church of Australia, alongside the 1978 *An Australian Prayer Book*, and the 1662 *Book of Common Prayer*

Accounts: the records of monies that the parish possesses, has received, or spent

Agenda: the order of business for a meeting

Anglican Church: the Anglican Church of Australia (*Parish Governance Act 2013* section 3)

Annual Meeting: each parish must hold a general, or main, meeting in either October or November each year

Apology: the prior notification given by someone unable to attend a meeting

Archdeacon: A senior priest who assists the bishop in a geographical area called an archdeaconry—in the Diocese of Melbourne, most archdeacons are also vicars with their own parishes

Archbishop: the chief ordained minister in the Diocese of Melbourne

Archbishop in Council: a body which meets throughout the year—it is the highest decision making body in the Diocese outside of the Synod and is made up of members elected by the Synod or appointed by the Archbishop directly

Area Dean: a priest who coordinates and supports other clergy and lay ministers in a geographical area known as a deanery, mainly for the purposes of meeting together for mutual support, prayer and encouragement

Assessment: the annual amount a parish must pay to the diocese from its funds (see *Parish Governance Act 2013*, sections 30–32)

Auditor: the professional accountant or accountants who check the parish accounts each year ahead of their presentation at the annual meeting (see *Parish Governance Act 2013*, section 44)

Authorised Anglican Congregation (AAC): a congregation, declared an AAC under the terms of the *Parish Governance Act 2013*, section 8, which is treated as though it were a parish.

Authorised Lay Minister: a lay (i.e. non-ordained) person who has been authorised by the Archbishop as a minister in a parish or other setting—Authorised Lay Ministers may be stipendiary, or paid, in which case they may be referred to as an Authorised Stipendiary Lay Minister (ASLM) or they may be honorary, or unpaid, and referred to as an Honorary Lay Minister (HLM)

Bishop: in the Diocese of Melbourne, the diocesan or chief bishop is the Archbishop, who is assisted by other bishops called Assistant Bishops, some of whom have responsibility for particular geographical areas known as 'areas of episcopal care'

Book of Common Prayer (BCP): the Prayer Book in use in the Church of England from the period of the Reformation, having its origins in the first edition of 1549 under the leadership of Archbishop (of Canterbury) Thomas Cranmer, and reaching its final state in 1662

Budget: the annual plan for raising and spending money

Canon: (i) the canons of the church, which are a series of rules and laws by which the church is governed (so, Canon Law); (ii) the clergy and laypeople who assist in the ministry of a cathedral

Cathedral: the principal place of worship in a diocese, in which the lead bishop, or Archbishop, has his 'cathedra' (seat or throne)

Chancellor: the senior legal officer in a diocese

Church: when applied to a building means a building of which the whole or some part is set apart and consecrated, or intended to be set apart and consecrated, exclusively for the worship of Almighty God according to the doctrine rites and usages of the Anglican Church (*Interpretation Act* 1878)

Churchwarden: the senior laypeople in a parish; two are elected each year by the annual meeting, and one is appointed by the vicar

Clergy/clergyperson/cleric: an ordained minister of the church—the clergy may be ordained as deacon, priest and bishop

Clerk in Holy Orders: a person who has been ordained in one or more of the three Orders of the church—deacon, priest, or bishop

Collect: a set prayer, prescribed for use on a particular day, also used in reference to a prayer said together by all; a collect gathers up, or 'collects' together, the prayers of all

Communicant member: a notoriously difficult term to define, it describes a person eligible to receive Holy Communion in an Anglican parish church

Curate: properly 'Assistant Curate'—an ordained person in the first few years of ministry, usually working under the supervision of another experienced clergyperson

Cure of souls: an old term, arising out of the *Book of Common Prayer*, to describe the pastoral function and ministry of a parish priest, reflecting its particular focus on the spiritual needs of those in the parish area

Deacon: one of the three orders of ministry in the Anglican Church; all clergy are ordained deacon, some may subsequently be ordained priest and bishop, whilst some remain deacons (often called 'distinctive deacons')

Dean: the priest in charge of a Cathedral (distinct from Area Dean—see p. 72)

Deanery: a geographical area within the diocese

Diocese: the geographical area under the oversight of a bishop or Archbishop

Ecclesiastical: a matter regarding or pertaining to the church, from *ekklesia*, the Greek word for 'church'

Electoral Roll: the list of laypeople entitled to vote at the annual meeting

Episcopal: means regarding the bishop or bishops, from the Greek *episkopos* meaning 'overseer'

Eucharist: an alternative term for the Holy Communion, from the Greek *eucharisteo* meaning 'thanksgiving'

Ex-officio: a person who is automatically a member of a body or council without having to be appointed or elected, usually by virtue of their position or office—ex-officio members of a parish council do not have the right to vote and cannot move or second motions, but may speak and contribute to the business of the meeting

Faculty: a document giving permission for something to be placed in a church, such as a memorial to a person, a fixture, decoration, or window—a faculty is also required to remove any such fixture for which a faculty has been previously obtained

Incumbency Committee: a body convened under the provisions of the *Appointments Act*; the incumbency committee is convened by the registrar, at the request of a bishop, if the parish becomes vacant, and sometimes if there is to be a review of the tenure of the vicar

Incumbent: a vicar whom the Archbishop has licensed to a parish as incumbent; the incumbent has tenure for up to ten years at the time of first being appointed to the parish, with the possibility of five-year extensions after the initial period of ten years

Independent Examiner: where the total receipts are less than $250,000 in a financial year, the parish may appoint an independent examiner instead of an auditor (see *Parish Governance Act 2013*, sections 46–47)

Interregnum: the period of time from the departure of one vicar and extending until the next vicar assumes office

Lay/layperson/laity: the people of a parish who are not ordained; from the Greek *laos* meaning 'people'

Liturgy: the words said, and actions performed, in a service of worship, and their sequence—usually as prescribed in a Prayer Book such as *A Prayer Book for Australia 1995*

Members of the Church: the members of the Anglican Church in the Diocese of Melbourne (*Interpretation Act* 1878)

Metropolitan: the bishop (designated an Archbishop) who is in charge of the largest diocese in a province—the Archbishop of Melbourne is the Metropolitan for the province of Victoria, which takes in the dioceses of Melbourne, Ballarat, Bendigo, Gippsland and Wangaratta

Minutes: the written record of a meeting

Parish: the geographical unit for organising the mission of God throughout the Anglican Church within the Diocese of Melbourne (*Parish Governance Act 2013* section 5)

Parish Electoral Committee: a committee formed annually to review the parish electoral roll, consisting of the vicar and either a churchwarden or a member of the parish council—*Parish Governance Act 2013*, section 10(1)

Parish officer: a person in a parish (other than the vicar) who is a churchwarden, member of the parish council, member of the incumbency committee, or member of a local vestry in a Section 18 parish (*Parish Governance Act 2013*, section 3)

Parish rules for meetings and officers: the rules referred to in Schedule One of the *Parish Governance Act 2013*

Parish secretary: the person appointed or elected as secretary under the parish rules for meetings and officers

Parish treasurer: the person appointed or elected as treasurer under the parish rules for meetings and officers

Parishioner: a person who is duly enrolled on a parish electoral roll under the provisions of the *Parish Governance Act 2013*

Parochial: pertaining to a parish

Polity: a form or process for governing a group or organisation—the rules, traditions, or body of legislation, often expressed in the context of a constitution or series of rules, by which a community, or an organisation, is governed

Priest: clergy ordained as a deacon may subsequently be ordained priest—in the Anglican Church some functions are reserved to priests who alone may pronounce absolution, give the blessing, and celebrate the Holy Communion

Priest in Charge (PiC): a clergyperson whom the Archbishop has licensed as priest-in-charge to a parish under the direction of the area bishop; the license is normally reviewed after three years

Quorum: the number of members that must be present in order for a meeting to proceed

Stewardship: in theological terms, means to take good and prudent care of the resources—financial, material, and other—entrusted to an individual, organisation or other entity

Stipend: a 'living'—the monies paid to an ordained clergyperson or authorised lay minister of the church (e.g. wages)

Synod: the highest decision making body of the diocese—Synod encompasses the licensed clergy together with the elected laypeople, and meets over three years, generally once in each year

Vacancy: a parish which has no vicar is said to be vacant or undergoing a vacancy

Verger (or Virger): a person appointed to assist with the smooth running of a church service, and/or to take care of the church and its grounds

Vestry: (i) the older term for the parish council; (ii) a room in the church where the clergy robe, or 'vest', and prepare for the service; (iii) the local governing body in a parish with more than one worship centre that has enacted section 18 of the *Parish Governance Act 2013*

Vicar: the priest in charge, the incumbent, or another cleric appointed temporarily by the Archbishop (called a locum) to act as such

Warden: see churchwarden

Appendix Two
A Treasury of Prayers

From *A Prayer Book for Australia* 1995

1. Before a meeting
> God our Creator,
> When you speak there is light and life.
> Fill us with your Holy Spirit
> So that we may listen to one another,
> Speak the truth in love,
> and bear much fruit in the service of your kingdom,
> through Jesus Christ our Lord. Amen.

2. In times of conflict
> God our refuge and strength,
> you have bound us together in a common life:
> help us, in the midst of our present conflict
> to confront one another without hatred or bitterness
> to listen for your voice amid competing claims
> and to work together with mutual forbearance and respect;
> through Jesus Christ our Lord. Amen.

3. Call to discipleship
> Christ, whose insistent call
> disturbs our settled lives:
> give us discernment or hear your word,

grace to relinquish our tasks,
and courage to follow empty-handed
wherever you may lead,
so that the voice of your gospel
may reach to the ends of the earth. Amen.

4. For God's guidance

Almighty and everlasting God,
direct, sanctify, and govern
our hearts and bodies in the ways of your law
and the works of your commandments.
By your mighty protection
may we be kept safe in body and soul
and serve you with generous and joyful hearts,
bringing glory to your holy name;
through our Lord and Savour Jesus Christ. Amen.

5. Dedication festival

Bountiful God,
to whose glory we celebrate the dedication of this house of prayer:
we praise you for the many blessings
you have given to those who worship here,
and we pray that all who seek you in this place may find you,
and being filled with the Holy Spirit
may become a living temple acceptable to you,
through Jesus Christ our Lord. Amen.

6. For the Church

Almighty God, we praise you for the blessings
brought to the world through your Church.
We bless you for the grace of the sacraments,

for our fellowship in Christ
with you and with each other,
for the teaching of the Scriptures,
and for the preaching of your word.
We thank you for the example of your saints,
for your faithful servants departed this life,
and for the memory of all that has been true
and good in their lives.
Number us with them
in the company of the redeemed of heaven;
through Jesus Christ our Lord. Amen.

7. The Grace

The grace of the Lord Jesus Christ,
And the love of God,
And the fellowship of the Holy Spirit,
Be with us all evermore. Amen.

8. Grace

Go before us, O Lord, in all our doings
with your most gracious favour,
and assist us with your continual help;
that in all works, begun, continued and ended in you,
we may glorify your holy name,
and finally by your mercy
obtain everlasting life;
through Jesus Christ our Lord. Amen.

9. The Lord's Prayer

Our Father in heaven,
hallowed be your name,

your kingdom come,
your will be done
on earth as in heaven.
Give us today our daily bread.
Forgive us our sins
as we forgive those who sin against us.
Save us from the time of trial,
and deliver us from evil.
For the kingdom, the power, and the glory are yours
now and forever. Amen.

From the *Book of Common Prayer*

10. The Prayer of General Thanksgiving

ALMIGHTY God, Father of all mercies, we thine unworthy servants do give thee most humble and hearty thanks for all thy goodness and loving-kindness to us, and to all men. We bless thee for our creation, preservation, and all the blessings of this life; but above all, for thine inestimable love in the redemption of the world by our Lord Jesus Christ; for the means of grace, and for the hope of glory. And, we beseech thee, give us that due sense of all thy mercies, that our hearts may be unfeignedly thankful, and that we shew forth thy praise, not only with our lips, but in our lives; by giving up ourselves to thy service, and by walking before thee in holiness and righteousness all our days; through Jesus Christ our Lord, to whom with thee and the Holy Ghost be all honour and glory, world without end. Amen.

11. The Second Collect at Evening Prayer

O GOD, from whom all holy desires, all good counsels, and all just works do proceed; give unto thy servants that peace which the world cannot give; that our hearts may be set to obey thy commandments, and also that by thee, we, being defended from the fear of our enemies, may pass our time in rest and quietness; through the merits of Jesus Christ our Saviour. Amen.

12. A Prayer of St Chrysostom

ALMIGHTY God, who hast given us grace at this time with one accord to make our common supplications unto thee; and dost promise, that when two or three are gathered together in thy Name thou wilt grant their requests; Fulfil now, O Lord, the desires and petitions of thy servants, as may be most expedient for them; granting us in this world knowledge of thy truth, and in the world to come life everlasting. Amen.

13. For the Holy Spirit's guidance

O GOD, forasmuch as without thee we are not able to please thee: mercifully grant that thy Holy Spirit may in all things direct and rule our hearts; through Jesus Christ our Lord. Amen.

14. For all our works

DIRECT us, O Lord, in all our doings, with thy most gracious favour, and further us with thy continual help; that in all our works begun, continued, and ended in thee, we may glorify thy holy Name, and finally, by thy mercy, obtain everlasting life; through Jesus Christ our Lord. Amen.[14]

From *Common Worship*, the Church of England

15. A Prayer for the Parish council

Almighty God,

---

14 *Book of Common Prayer*, 1928.

you have given your Holy Spirit to the Church
to lead us into all truth;
bless with the Spirit's grace and presence the members of this
Parish council;
keep us steadfast in faith and united in love,
that we may manifest your glory
and prepare the way for your kingdom;
through Jesus Christ, your Son our Lord. Amen.

16. For guidance
Almighty God,
we thank you for the gift of your holy word.
May it be a lantern to our feet,
a light to our paths,
and a strength to our lives.
Take us and use us
to love and serve
in the power of the Holy Spirit
and in the name of your Son,
Jesus Christ our Lord. Amen.

Prayers from other places

17. Before a meeting (i)
Living God,
as we meet in Council today may we meet with you.
Grant us wisdom, patience, and courage
as you shape our conversation, our thinking, and our deciding.
Guide our thoughts to embrace the overlooked and forgotten;
lift our hearts to desire earnestly the highest good for all;
and draw our decisions to conform to the purpose of your will.

In Christ our Lord and master we pray. Amen.[15]

18. Before a meeting (ii)

O Lord, we meet in your name and we ask most humbly that your spirit of wisdom and understanding may direct and rule our hearts, and all that we do and all we say may be to your glory and to the furtherance of your kingdom, and that in all things we may be faithful servants of your Son, our Saviour Jesus Christ. Amen.[16]

19. For wisdom

If any of you is lacking in wisdom, ask God, who gives to all generously and ungrudgingly, and it will be given you. But ask in faith, never doubting, for the one who doubts is like a wave of the sea, driven and tossed by the wind. (James 1.5–6)

Lord,
your word says that when we lack wisdom we should ask,
and in asking believe,
and in believing receive.
We need, and we lack,
so we ask, and we trust…
Give us wisdom we pray,
in and through Christ our Lord. Amen.[17]

20. Prayers of gratitude and concern

For the roots of our community,

---

15 Mark Tanner, *The PCC Member's Essential Guide: A beginners guide to hold on to!* (London: Church House Publishing, 2015), p. 43.
16 Pat Robson, *A Celtic Liturgy* (London: HarperCollins, 2000), p. 81.
17 Mark Tanner, *The PCC Member's Essential Guide: A beginners guide to hold on to!* (London: Church House Publishing, 2015), p. 56.

and for all communities:
we thank you, Living God.
For what we share together,
and for the life we share with others:
we thank you, Living God.
For the path that lies before us now,
and our future in your hands:
we thank you, Living God.

Further prayers may be offered...
O Christ, you are within each of us.
It is not just the interior of these walls:
it is our own inner being you have renewed.
We are your temple not made with hands.
We are your body.
If every wall should crumble, and every church decay,
we are your habitation.
Nearer are you than breathing,
closer than hands and feet.
Ours are the eyes with which you, in the mystery,
look out with compassion on the world.
Yet we bless you for this place,
for your directing of us, your redeeming of us,
and your indwelling.
Take us outside, O Christ, outside holiness,
out to where soldiers curse and nations clash,
at the crossroads of the world.
So shall this building continue to be justified.
We ask it for your own name's sake. Amen.[18]

---

18 The Iona Community. *Iona Abbey Worship Book* (Glasgow: Wild Goose Publications, 2001), p. 28.

21. A short litany

Let us pray.
Guide us, Lord, by your Holy Spirit, so that this parish council may promote your work among us and build up your holy church.
Lord, in your mercy, **Hear our prayer.**
Direct all our discussion and debate, so that we may discern your will for us and make right decisions on the matters before us.
Lord, in your mercy, **Hear our prayer.**
Keep our focus on your commands and promises to us, so that we may be bold in our mission to the people of this community.
Lord, in your mercy, **Hear our prayer.**
Make us ready to listen, slow to criticise, and willing to cooperate with each other, so that we may promote the unity which you have given us.
Lord, in your mercy, **Hear our prayer.**
Encourage and inspire us through this meeting, so that we may be better equipped to serve you as your priestly people; through your Son Jesus Christ our Lord, who lives and reigns with you and the Holy Spirit, one God, now and for ever. Amen.[19]

22. For modesty

Grant unto us, O Lord, the gift of modesty.
When we speak, teach us to give our opinion quietly and sincerely.
When we do well in work or play, give us a sense of proportion, that we be neither unduly elated nor foolishly self-deprecatory.
Help us in success to realise what we owe to thee and to the efforts of others:
in failure, to avoid dejection;
and in all ways to be simple and natural,

---

19 Prayer for the opening of a synodical convention (adapted), from *Church Rites* (The Lutheran Church of Australia, 1994), pp. 257–258.

quiet in manner and lowly in thought:
through Christ. Amen.[20]

23. When we disagree

Father, this is hard but you understand.
Calm us, we pray, that we might attend to the still, small voice…
… the silent echo of your presence
… the echo of your goodness and grace
… the breath of life that you breathe over each of us
… and the echoing cries of a needy world.
Blow away our anger, fear, confusion, and all that clouds our vision,
and renew our love, our hope, our peace, and even, we pray, our joy.
Rest upon us, Spirit of the Living God,
and grant us a gentle heart and grace-filled mind…
… the very mind of Christ. Amen.[21]

24. To the Holy Spirit

O Holy Spirit,
giver of light and life,
impart to us thoughts higher than our own thoughts,
and prayers better than our own prayers,
and powers beyond our own powers,
that we may spend and be spent
in the ways of love and goodness,
after the perfect image
of our Lord and Saviour Jesus Christ. Amen.[22]

---

20 George Appleton (Ed), *The Oxford Book of Prayer* (Oxford: Oxford University Press, 1985), p. 122.
21 Mark Tanner, *The PCC Member's Essential Guide: A beginners guide to hold on to!* (London: Church House Publishing, 2015), p. 29.
22 A prayer of Eric Milner-White (1884–1964), in George Appleton (Ed), *The Oxford Book of Prayer* (Oxford: Oxford University Press, 1985), p. 155.

25. For the enlightenment of the mind

    Enlighten us, O good Jesus,
    with the brightness of internal light,
    and cast out all darkness
    from the dwelling of our hearts.
    Grant us, O Lord,
    to know that which is worth knowing,
    to love what is worth loving
    to praise that which can bear with praise,
    to hate what in your sight is unworthy,
    to prize what to you is precious,
    and above all, to search and do your holy will. Amen.[23]

26. For illumination

    Most gracious God, our heavenly Father,
    in you alone dwells all fullness of light and wisdom:
    illuminate our minds by the Holy Spirit
    in the true understanding of your Word.
    Give us grace that we may receive it
    with sincere reverence and humility.
    May it lead us to put our whole trust in you alone;
    and so to serve and honour you
    that we may glorify your name,
    and encourage others by the good example
    of a holy life.
    And because it has pleased you to number us
    among your people,
    help us to give you the love and homage that we owe,
    as children of the light and as servants to our Lord.

---

[23] A prayer of Thomas á Kempis (1380–1471), in *Uniting in Worship* (Melbourne: The Uniting Church in Australia, 1988), p. 218.

We ask this for the sake of our Master and Saviour. Amen.[24]

27. For the knowledge of God's will
Almighty and everlasting God,
in whom we live and move and have our being,
who hast created us for thyself,
so that we can find rest only in thee;
grant unto us such purity of heart
and strength of purpose,
that no selfish passion may hinder us
from knowing thy will,
no weakness from doing it;
but in thy light we may see light clearly,
and in thy service find perfect freedom;
for Jesus Christ's sake. Amen.[25]

28. Instruments of peace
Lord, make us instruments of your peace.
Where there is hatred, let us sow love;
where there is injury, pardon;
where there is discord, union;
where there is doubt, faith;
where there is despair, hope;
where there is darkness, light;
where there is sadness, joy.
Grant that we may not so much seek
to be consoled as to console;
to be understood as to understand;
to be loved as to love.

---

24 A prayer of John Calvin (1509–1564), in *Uniting in Worship* (Melbourne: The Uniting Church in Australia, 1988), p. 220.
25 The Church of Scotland, *Book of Common Order*, 1940.

> For it is in giving that we receive;
> it is in pardoning that we are pardoned;
> and it is in dying that we are born to eternal life. Amen.[26]

29. Closing a meeting

> O Lord, we offer you the thoughts and deliberations of this meeting, and we ask that you forgive our shortcomings and our lack of understanding. May we be mindful of your trust and ready always to work in harmony with each other, that through us your kingdom may go forward and your will be done. Amen.[27]

30. A Blessing

> May the love of the Lord Jesus
> draw us to himself;
> may the power of the Lord Jesus
> strengthen us in his service;
> may the joy of the Lord Jesus
> fill our souls.
> May the blessing of God Almighty,
> the Father, the Son, and the Holy Ghost,
> be amongst us
> and remain with us
> always. Amen.[28]

Prayers for personal use

31. For people I find difficult

> Lord Jesus,

---

26 Attributed to St Francis of Assisi (1182–1226).
27 Pat Robson, *A Celtic Liturgy* (London: HarperCollins, 2000), p. 81.
28 A prayer of William Temple (1881–1944), in George Appleton (Ed), *The Oxford Book of Prayer* (Oxford: Oxford University Press, 1985), p. 172.

I bring N. before you:

your hands 'knit them together' and you know all their days and all their ways,

thank you for your extraordinary love for them,

and that when I reflect on you loving them,

I grow in my trust that you can actually love the real me too:

let that love fill us,

transform us,

renew us,

that I may truly pray for them and be grateful for their prayer for me,

and that together we may see your goodness at work in us and through us,

for you are the God of all goodness and transforming love. Amen.[29]

32. For when we are nervous about something we have to say or do
Jesus said, 'Peace be with you! As the Father has sent me, I am sending you.' And with that he breathed on them and said, 'Receive the Holy Spirit.' (John 20.21-22)

Lord Jesus, I receive your peace...

I receive not because I have earned, or practiced, or invested,

but because you promise and you are faithful.

Lord Jesus, I go because you were sent and now you send me...

I might not get it all right, but please guide me to get it right enough.

Protect me from my weakness, and, release me in your strength,

and let the glory be yours.

Lord, I receive your Spirit as you breathe upon me...

---

[29] Mark Tanner, *The PCC Member's Essential Guide: A beginners guide to hold on to!* (London: Church House Publishing, 2015), p. 29.

unite your Spirit with my own,
transforming me, renewing me, commissioning me, and using me, to your glory,
loving others, and in the service of your coming kingdom. Amen.[30]

33. When I don't understand
O God of wisdom and understanding,
thank you that you know what all of this means,
even when I have little or no idea!
Direct my eyes to the important things,
enlighten my mind with understanding,
help me to know the questions that need to be asked,
and give me peace to trust where I do not need to know.
In all of this, let your Kingdom come, your Name be glorified,
and your people be drawn to you, the God of all insight and grace. Amen.[31]

34. The serenity prayer
God, grant me the serenity to accept the things I cannot change,
Courage to change the things I can,
And wisdom to know the difference.[32]

---

30 Mark Tanner, *The PCC Member's Essential Guide: A beginners guide to hold on to!* (London: Church House Publishing, 2015), p. 33.
31 *The PCC Member's Essential Guide: A beginners guide to hold on to!* (London: Church House Publishing, 2015), p. 61.
32 Reinhold Niebuhr (1892–1971).

APPENDIX THREE
FURTHER RESOURCES

Online

Synod legislation—Anglican Diocese of Melbourne (via the Parish Portal—login required)
- https://parishportal.melbourneanglican.org.au/library/pages/synod-legislation.aspx

Constitution & Canons of the Anglican Church of Australia
- http://www.anglican.org.au/governance/pages/constitution.aspx

Anglican Diocese of Melbourne
- http://www.melbourneanglican.org.au/Pages/Anglican-Diocese-of-Melbourne.aspx

The Bishop Perry Institute for Mission and Ministry
- http://www.bishopperryinstitute.org.au

Anglican Church of Australia
- http://www.anglican.org.au/home/Pages/welcome.aspx

Anglican Communion
- http://www.anglicancommunion.org/identity/about.aspx

Australian Bureau of Statistics—for finding data for local government areas
- http://www.abs.gov.au/websitedbs/D3310114.nsf/Home/Finding+data+for+Local+Government+areas

In print

Avis, Paul. *The Anglican understanding of the Church: An introduction.* London: SPCK, 2013.

Bayes, Paul & Tim Sledge. *Mission-Shaped parish: traditional church in a changing context.* London: Church House Publishing, 2009.

Chapman, Mark. *Anglicanism: A very short Introduction.* Oxford: Oxford University Press, 2006.

Davis, John. *Australian Anglicans and their Constitution.* Canberra: Acorn Press, 1993.

Giles, Kevin. *Making good churches better: A workbook for Church councils and Church leaders.* Melbourne: Acorn Press, 2001.

Grant, James. *Episcopally led and Synodically governed: Anglicans in Victoria 1803–1997.* Melbourne: Australian Scholarly Publishing, 2010.

Hale, Stephen & Andrew Curnow (Eds). *Facing the future: Bishops imagine a different Church.* Melbourne: Acorn, 2009.

Ison, David (Ed). *The vicar's guide: Life and ministry in the parish.* London: Church House Publishing, 2008.

Jackson, Bob. *Hope for the Church: Contemporary strategies for growth.* London: Church House Publishing, 2002.

Kaye, Bruce. *A Church without walls: being Anglican in Australia.* Sydney: Dove, 1995.

Kaye, Bruce (Ed). *Anglicanism in Australia: A history.* Melbourne: Melbourne University Press, 2002.

Nichols, Alan (Ed). *Building the mission-Shaped Church in Australia: A resource book for churches, home groups and diocesan staff meetings with questions for small group discussion.* Sydney: The General Synod of the Anglican Church of Australia, 2006.

Tanner, Mark. *The PCC Member's Essential Guide: A beginners guide to hold on to!* London: Church House Publishing, 2015.

Warren, Robert. *The healthy churches' handbook.* London: Church House Publishing, 2004.

Appendix Four
The Parish Governance Act 2013

Note: the *Parish Governance Act 2013* includes amendments made by the Melbourne Anglican Diocesan Corporation Act 2015 that are yet to come into force.

No. 1 of 2013   Serial No. 218

(As in force October 2016, assuming proclamation of MADC Act)
Parish Governance Act 2013
AN ACT
to provide for the establishment, governance and Diocesan oversight of parishes and for other purposes

BE IT ENACTED by the Archbishop, the Clergy and the Laity of the Anglican Church of Australia within the Diocese of Melbourne in Victoria duly met in Synod according to law as follows:

PART 1—PRELIMINARY

1. Short title
This Act may be cited as the *Parish Governance Act 2013*.

2. Commencement
This Act comes into operation on 1 July 2014.

3. Definitions
(1) In this Act, unless the context otherwise requires—

accounting records includes:

(a) invoices, receipts, orders for the payment of money, bills of exchange, cheques, promissory notes, vouchers and other documents of prime entry;

(b) documents and records that record those entries;

(c) documents, records and communications showing the authorization or ratification of expenditure; and

(d) any working papers and other documents that are necessary to explain the methods and calculations by which accounts are made up;

accounts means a combination of:

(a) an account recording the total receipts and payments; and

(b) a statement of assets and liabilities—

together with any statements, reports and notes, other than the reports of an auditor or independent examiner, that are attached to and intended to be read with the account, statement or balance sheet, as the case may be;

Anglican Church means the Anglican Church of Australia;

annual diocesan assessment means the amount payable under section 30;

bankrupt includes a person who applies to take the benefit of any law for the relief of bankrupt or insolvent debtors, compounding with his or her creditors or making an assignment of his or her remuneration for their benefit;

Church has the same meaning as in section 7(2) of the *Interpretation Act 1878*;

diocesan authority means:

(a)   the Archbishop, whether or not acting with the advice and consent of the Council of the Diocese;

(b)   an Assistant Bishop;

(c)   an Archdeacon;

(d)   the Registrar.

Diocese means the Diocese of Melbourne;

Director of Professional Standards has the same meaning as Director in the *Professional Standards Act 2009*;

disqualified person means a person disqualified under section 19;

financial year means the year ending at midnight on 30 September;

local electoral roll means a roll showing only the parishioners on a parish electoral roll associated with a particular worship centre in the parish;

mental incapacity means a person who has a mental illness within the meaning of section 8 of the *Mental Health Act 1986* (Vic);

neighbouring parish means a parish that it is contiguous or nearby

parish council in relation to a parish, means the parish council established by the parish rules for meetings and officers;

parish electoral roll means the roll established under section 9;

parish officer includes a person in a parish (other than the vicar) who is a churchwarden, member of the parish council, member of the incumbency committee or member of a vestry;

parish rules for meetings and officers means the rules referred to in Division 2 of Part 4;

parish secretary means the parish secretary appointed or

elected under the parish's parish rules for meetings and officers;

statutory parish meeting means any annual meeting, special meeting, parish electoral meeting, special parish electoral meeting, or meeting of parishioners on a local electoral roll provided for in this Act, the regulations or a parish's parish rules for meetings and officers;

vestry in relation to a worship centre means the vestry established by the parish's parish rules for meetings and officers;

vicar means:

(a) the incumbent;

(b) a clerk appointed temporarily by the Archbishop to perform the ecclesiastical duties of the incumbency;

(c) if there is no incumbent and no clerk appointed under paragraph (b), or if such a person is absent from the parish on leave, the Archdeacon;

worship centre means a place within the parish used regularly by the parish for public worship, and includes a principal worship centre and a local worship centre.

(2) For the purposes of this Act and any regulations made under this Act and the parish rules for meetings and officers of any parish, ***communicant member*** means a person who is on the parish electoral roll and who is eligible to be admitted to Holy Communion under the Admission to Holy Communion Canon 1973 of the General Synod of the Anglican Church.

> Note: Section 3 of the Reception Canon 1981 of the General Synod of the Anglican Church provides that a person received into communicant membership in accordance with that canon has the same status in the

Anglican Church of Australia as a person who has been confirmed in accordance with the rites of that Church.

(3) For the purpose of this Act, ***principal worship centre*** means the principal place of worship referred to in section 8, and ***local worship centre*** means a worship centre within the parish other than the principal worship centre or a worship centre that is with the prior approval of the Archbishop in Council under section 8(4) associated with the parish.

(4) Where in this Act it is provided that a parish must do an act, it is the churchwardens who must seek in good faith to ensure that the parish does that act.

(5) In this Act, other than in sections 19(3), 21(7), 27(4), 28, 29, 37(3), 37(4), 38(5), 40, 54(1), 55, 61(3), 62(1), and 72(1), a reference to the Archbishop in relation to any matter pertaining to the temporal affairs of the church means the Archbishop acting with the consent of the Council of the Diocese.

(6) In this Act other than section 4, a reference to a diocesan authority includes a reference to a person acting as the delegate or agent of a diocesan authority.

4. Delegation

(1) A diocesan authority other than the Archbishop in Council may delegate to any person or body any of its powers under this Act, other than this power of delegation.

(2) The Archbishop in Council may delegate to any person or body (including to the Archbishop) any of its powers under this Act, other than the power to make regulations, including the power of delegation.

(3) A delegation may be withdrawn in whole or in part, varied, or given again to the same or some other person.

(4) A delegation given to a person may be given to them by name or by reference to an office or position.

(5) Where a delegation has been given to a person by reference to an office or position, the delegated power may be exercised by anyone for the time being occupying or acting in that office or position.

(6) A delegation, variation to a delegation or withdrawal of a delegation must be in writing and has effect from the time at which it is given to the Registry for registration.

PART 2—THE PARISH

5. The Anglican understanding of a parish

The parish is the geographical unit for organizing the mission of God throughout the Anglican Church within the Diocese of Melbourne. The boundaries of each parish are those approved by the Archbishop in Council. The Anglican Church within the Diocese is constituted of clergy and lay people committed to building up the body of Christ under the leadership of the Archbishop.

PART 3—ESTABLISHING A PARISH AND DEFINING ITS BOUNDARIES

6. Declaration of parishes

The Archbishop in Council may declare that there is a parish in relation to a geographical area within the Diocese.

7. Parish boundaries

(1) When—

    (a) declaring a part of the Diocese not included in a parish to be a parish;

    (b) dividing a parish into separate parishes;

    (c) creating a parish from more than one existing parish;

(d) altering the boundaries of parishes under sub-section (3), or

(e) merging parishes or discontinuing a parish under Division 3 of Part 7—

the Archbishop in Council must by words of description with or without maps or plans declare in writing the boundaries of every parish affected.

(2) Before the Archbishop in Council can divide a parish into separate parishes or create a parish from more than one existing parish, it must have before it a written report as to the views regarding the proposal expressed by the vicar, the parish officers and a statutory parish meeting of the parish or each of the parishes directly affected, including their views in relation to the proposed new boundaries.

(3) Where it is proposed that the boundaries of two or more parishes be altered such that no more than 25 per cent of the area of any parish will be added or removed, and the vicar and parish officers of all affected parishes agree in writing to the proposal, the Archbishop in Council may alter the boundaries of those parishes in the manner proposed.

(4) Every declaration made under sub-section (1) must be preserved in the Registry of the Diocese.

(5) The Registrar must if so requested provide the description of a parish referred to in sub-section (1).

(6) A declaration under sub-section (1) is conclusive evidence of the boundaries of a parish.

8. Places of worship

(1) A parish must have a principal place of worship.

(2) If a parish has more than one worship centre, the principal worship centre is the worship centre so designated by the Archbishop in Council.

(3) Unless otherwise authorized by the Archbishop in Council, the principal place of worship must be a building of which the whole or some part is set apart and consecrated or intended to be set apart and consecrated exclusively for the worship of Almighty God according to the doctrine, rites and usages of the Anglican Church.

(4) The Archbishop in Council may permit a parish to conduct public worship in a worship centre outside the parish's boundaries.

(5) Before giving its permission under sub-section (4), the Archbishop in Council must be informed of the views of the parish in which the worship centre is placed, and of the relevant Archdeacon.

PART 3A—AUTHORISED ANGLICAN CONGREGATIONS
8A. *Initial formation of congregations*

(1) The Archbishop in Council may permit those wishing to participate in the initial formation of a congregation that may later be declared an Authorised Anglican Congregation under section 8B to do so is satisfied that the relevant Archdeacon and the parish or parishes immediately affected have been consulted.

(2) The Archbishop may license a clerk to a congregation formed under this section.

8B. *Declaration of Authorised Anglican Congregation*

(1) The Archbishop in Council may declare a congregation that meets each of the criteria in sub-section (2) to be an Authorised Anglican Congregation.

(2) The criteria are—
    (a) there is a congregation (not being the congregation

of a parish) the members of which meet regularly for public worship as an Anglican congregation;

(b) the congregation has a vision and mission that define its ministry goals as an Anglican congregation;

(c) the place where the congregation conducts public worship is a suitable place set aside for the regular use of the congregation, whether under a lease, licence or other arrangement;

(d) the incumbent and council of each parish wholly or partly within the area proposed to be determined under sub-section (3)(a) have been fully consulted regarding the proposed declaration of the congregation as an Authorised Anglican Congregation;

(e) a name acceptable to the congregation has been proposed for the purposes of sub-section (3)(b);

(f) in all the circumstances and in furtherance of the mission of the church it is appropriate to recognize the congregation as an Authorised Anglican Congregation; and

(g) the Archbishop has expressed a willingness to license a priest in charge to that congregation (who may be a priest already ministering to or licensed to the congregation).

(3) At the time of making a declaration under sub-section (1) the Archbishop in Council must determine—

(a) a geographic area within which the congregation is permitted to meet for the purposes of worship, to maintain offices and similar premises, and to locate the residence of the priest licensed to that congregation;

(b) a name, determined in accordance with the current policy of the Archbishop in Council for the naming of parishes, to be used by the congregation in its official correspondence and in its publicity and advertising;
(c) the archdeaconry of which the congregation is part;
(d) if, and if so on what terms and conditions, the diocesan assessment is to be waived, in whole or in part, under section 32.

(4) The Archbishop in Council may from time to time as necessary vary a determination made under sub-section (3).

8C. Periodic review

(1) The Archbishop in Council must review the operations of an Authorised Anglican Congregation against the criteria in section 8B(2) and any other criteria in the guidelines adopted under section 8F at a time no more than five years from the date of making a declaration under section 8B(1), and thereafter at an interval of not more than five years since the last such review.

(2) A review under sub-section (1) may result in the Archbishop in Council varying a determination under section 8D(1) or revoking a declaration under section 8D(2).

8D. Varying and revoking determinations and declarations

(1) The Archbishop in Council may from time to time as necessary vary a determination made under sub-section (3).

(2) The Archbishop in Council may revoke a declaration made under sub-section (1).

(3) Before varying a determination or revoking a declaration under this section, the Archbishop in Council must have regard to—

(a) any periodic review under section 8C and any recommendations contained in or arising from that review;

(b) the views of the priest in charge and council of the Authorised Anglican Congregation in relation to the proposed decision;

(c) the matters referred to in sub-section 72(2) (excluding paragraph (e)); and

(d) the guidelines made under section 8E.

(4) The revocation of a declaration under sub-section (2) may be made in association with a decision in relation to a declaration under section 6 or 7.

8E. Guidelines

The Archbishop in Council must make and publish guidelines relating to the administration of this Part.

8F. Application of certain Acts of Synod

(1) This Act except for—

    (a) Parts 2 and 3;

    (b) section 18; and

    (c) Division 3 of Part 7 (other than section 71)—

applies to an Authorised Anglican Congregation as if the Authorised Anglican Congregation were a parish.

(2) Despite sub-section (1), in relation to an Authorised Anglican Congregation the Parish Governance Act 2013 and any regulations and rules made under it is to be read and interpreted as if in that Act—

(a) the expression "congregation council" is substituted for the expression "parish council";

(b) the expression "wardens" is substituted for the expression "churchwardens"; and

(c) the expression "incumbent" means the clerk instituted as priest in charge of the Authorised Anglican Congregation.

(3) Part II and Part IV of the Appointments Act 1971 have effect so far as applicable for the purpose of enabling an Authorised Anglican Congregation to propose a priest as its priest in charge and as if a reference in that Part—

(a) to an incumbent, or an incumbency, were a reference to a priest in charge or the position of a priest in charge; and

(b) to a parish were a reference to the Authorised Anglican Congregation."

(4) Part II and Part IV of the **Appointments Act 1971** have effect so far as applicable for the purpose of enabling an Authorised Anglican Congregation to propose a priest as its priest in charge and as if a reference in that Part—

(a) to an incumbent, or an incumbency, were a reference to a priest in charge or the position of a priest in charge; and

(b) to a parish were a reference to the Authorised Anglican Congregation.

PART 4—PARISH GOVERNMENT

Division 1—Electoral rolls

9. *Persons entitled to be on the parish electoral roll*

(1) There must be a parish electoral roll for each parish.

(2) A person is not entitled to be upon the roll of more than one parish or Authorised Anglican Congregation, or upon the roll of a parish and an Authorised Anglican Congregation.

(3) The parish electoral roll is to contain the names and postal

addresses of parishioners. Parishioners are laypersons who are of at least eighteen years of age and who—

(a) are baptised;
(b) regularly and habitually attend public worship at a worship centre in the parish;
(c) have signed an application seeking to be included on the roll and declaring that—
   (i) they are a member of the Anglican Church of Australia or of a church in communion with the Anglican Church of Australia;
   (ii) they are not a member of any church which is not in communion with the Anglican Church of Australia; and
   (iii) they are not on the parish electoral roll of any other parish or any Authorised Anglican Congregation in the Diocese other than a roll from which they wish their name to be removed.

(4) Without limiting other grounds on which a person may be taken to have regularly and habitually attended public worship in a worship centre in a parish, for the purposes of this section a person who has attended public worship at a worship centre 12 times in the preceding 12 months and three times in the preceding three months is considered to have regularly and habitually attended public worship at that worship centre.

(5) Where there is more than one worship centre in a parish, the parish electoral roll must show in respect of each parishioner a worship centre with which they are associated.

(6) The worship centre with which a parishioner is shown as being associated for the purposes of sub-section (5) is a worship centre at which the parishioner regularly and

habitually attends public worship that has for the purposes of the roll been—
(a) identified by the parishioner; or
(b) if not so identified, determined by the parish electoral committee—

as the worship centre with which the parishioner is associated.

10. *Forming a parish electoral roll*

(1) For each parish there is a parish electoral committee consisting of the vicar and a churchwarden or member of the parish council appointed by the parish council at its first meeting after the annual meeting.

(2) Where the Archbishop in Council declares a new parish and there is in relation to that parish under the *Trustees Act 1910*—
 (a) a Provisional Committee, the vicar and the Provisional Committee constitute the parish electoral committee in that parish until there is a parish electoral committee; and
 (b) a Secretary, the Secretary is the parish secretary under this Division until there is a parish secretary.

(3) When it declares a new parish and Part II of the *Trustees Act 1910* does not apply, the Archbishop in Council must—
 (a) establish an interim parish electoral committee to perform the functions of a parish electoral committee in that parish until there is a parish electoral committee; and
 (b) appoint a person to perform the functions of the parish secretary under this Division until there is a parish secretary.

11. Revising the parish electoral roll

(1) The parish electoral roll must be maintained and revised by the parish electoral committee.

(2) Subject to sub-section (3), the parish electoral roll must be revised and if necessary amended each year so as to be completed at a time between 15 and 28 days before the annual meeting of the parish or worship centre to which the roll relates to add the names of people eligible to be on it and to remove the names of people who have become ineligible.

(3) The parish roll may not be amended—
   (a) in the period of 14 days preceding the annual meeting; or
   (b) during the period between the time when the churchwardens fix the date of a statutory parish meeting (other than an annual meeting) and the conclusion of that meeting.

(4) At least 14 days before the revision referred to in sub-section 2, notice must be given as widely as possible within the parish of the revision.

(5) The name of a parishioner must not be removed only on the grounds that they have not regularly and habitually attended public worship at a worship centre in the parish during the previous three months if they have failed to attend for some temporary or unavoidable reason.

12. Display and inspection of the electoral roll

(1) Subject to this section, the parish electoral roll revised and amended in accordance with section 11(2) must be dated, signed and certified by the parish electoral committee and displayed clearly, together with any names that have been removed since the last annual meeting—
   (a) near the main entrance to each church in the parish throughout the 14 days preceding the annual meeting; and

(b) in a place and manner obvious to anyone attending public worship in a worship centre that is not a church during, and for a reasonable time before and after, each occasion of public worship in that worship centre in the 14 days preceding the annual meeting.

(2) Subject to this section, anyone who is on the parish electoral roll may inspect the roll at any time at no charge by request to the parish secretary.

(3) A copy of the parish electoral roll displayed under sub-section (1) must be presented to the annual meeting of the parish and must be provided to the Registrar by the parish secretary if the Registrar so requests.

(4) The parish electoral roll or local electoral roll that is publicly displayed or available for inspection must not show any information other than that person's first name and surname unless the person has agreed in writing for that other information to be available for public display and inspection.

13. People moving between parishes

(1) If a person applies to be on the electoral roll of a parish and wishes to be removed from the electoral roll of another parish, the parish secretary must inform the parish secretary of that other parish of the person's wish.

(2) Once an electoral roll of the other parish has been amended by removing a name as a result of a notice received under sub-section (1), the parish secretary of the other parish must inform the parish secretary of the new parish that the amendment has been made.

14. Prescribed forms for the purpose of this Division

The Archbishop in Council may prescribe forms that are to be used for the purposes of applications, notices and other communications required by this Division.

Appendix Four The Parish Governance Act 2013

Division 2—Parish rules for meetings and officers

15. Parish rules for meetings and officers

(1) The parish rules for meetings and officers in Schedule 1 apply to each parish.

(2) If section 18 applies to a parish, the additional rules in Schedule 2 apply to that parish.

(3) Where in Schedule 1 provision is made for an alternative or additional rule, the parish may by following the procedures in section 16 adopt that rule as part of the parish's modified parish rules for meetings and officers.

16. Modified parish rules for meetings and officers

(1) Modified parish rules for meetings and officers may be proposed by—

   (a) three churchwardens;
   (b) the parish council; or
   (c) 10 or more parishioners.

(2) A statutory parish meeting may adopt modified parish rules for meetings and officers only to the extent that—

   (a) the text is permitted text in Schedule 1; and
   (b) the permitted text is used in conformity with the instructions corresponding to that text in Schedule 1.

(3) A statutory parish meeting may not adopt or amend modified parish rules for meetings and officers at a time when there is no incumbent or when the incumbent is under suspension from the duties of the office.

(4) Before a statutory parish meeting may adopt modified parish rules for meetings and officers under sub-section (2)—

   (a) at least one month's notice of the meeting must have been given; and
   (b) the full text of the proposed modified parish rules for

meetings and officers must have been always available during the period of one month before the meeting.

(5) If at a meeting to adopt modified parish rules for meetings and officers, or at any meeting adjourned under this sub-section—
  (a) it is moved and seconded that the rules as available before the meeting be amended in any way; and
  (b) following the consideration of all such motions one or more such motions has been carried—
the meeting must be adjourned for at least 14 days to a date fixed and announced by the Chair before the meeting is adjourned for the further consideration of the motion to adopt the modified rules.

(6) A parish may further modify its parish rules for meetings and officers by following the procedure set out in sub-sections (1), (2), (3), (4) and (5).

(7) Modified or further modified parish rules for meetings and officers may be expressed to come into effect on any date or at any time not more than 14 months after the meeting at which they are adopted.

(8) The parish must provide a copy of modified and further modified parish rules for meetings and officers to the Registrar as soon as they have been adopted.

(9) Subject to sub-section (10), the Registrar must register the modified or further modified rules and notify the parish that they have been registered.

(10) The Registrar—
  (a) must not register a parish's modified or further modified parish rules for meetings and officers unless satisfied that they contain no modifications other than those allowed by Schedule 1; and

(b) if in doubt as to whether modified or further modified rules contain only modifications allowed by Schedule 1, must refer the modified or further modified rules to the Archbishop in Council for a final determination as to whether they may be registered.

(11) The Archbishop in Council must not determine that a parish's modified or further modified parish rules for meetings and officers referred to it under sub-section (10) may be registered unless it is satisfied that they contain only modifications allowed by Schedule 1.

(12) The Registrar must register the modified parish rules for meetings and officers and notify the parish that they have been registered.

(13) If modified or further modified parish rules for meetings and officers are registered, they have effect from the date on which they are registered under sub-sections (9) or (12) or on the date or at the time expressed in the modified rules, whichever is the later.

(14) Subject to sub-section (15), the modified parish rules for meetings and officers, whether or not further modified, cease to have effect on the earlier of—

(a) the date fixed for that purpose by the modified rules; or

(b) the end of the annual meeting of the parish held in the tenth year after the meeting that adopted the modified rules.

(15) If at the time when modified parish rules for meetings and officers are to cease to have effect under sub-section (14) the parish has no incumbent, they continue to have effect until the end of the first statutory parish meeting held after the institution of the next incumbent.

(16) A parish must state in its annual statistical return whether it

has modified parish rules for meetings and officers and the date on which those rules cease to have effect by virtue of sub-section (14).

(17) In this section, **modified parish rules for meetings and officers** means the rules in Schedule 1 varied in accordance sub-section (2).

17. Rules applying to elections

(1) An election at a statutory parish meeting must be conducted so as to fill the offices and positions provided for in the parish rules for meetings and officers that will be in place following the close of that meeting.

(2) Where—
   (a) an election or appointment is to take place at a statutory parish meeting, and
   (b) the parish rules for meetings and officers that will operate in relation to the election or the offices following the meeting are different from those operating up to the end of the meeting—

   the meeting may resolve—

   (c) that the meeting stand adjourned for a period not exceeding 21 days; and
   (d) that the election or appointment is to take place at that adjourned meeting—

   and may further set a closing date for the receipt of additional nominations for election.

18. Parishes with a local worship centre

(1) If there is a local worship centre in a parish, the parishioners on the local electoral roll of that local worship centre may at a meeting called for the purpose resolve that this section applies.

(2) If this section applies—

(a) the budget presented to the annual meeting of the parish must include details of the income from each worship centre and the expenditure associated with the buildings and accommodation of each worship centre; and

(b) a meeting of the parishioners on the local electoral roll of one or more of:

   (i) the principal worship centre; and

   (ii) a local worship centre—

may resolve that there is to be a local annual meeting for that worship centre and, if it resolves that there is to be an annual meeting for that worship centre, that there is to be a vestry for that worship centre.

(3) A local statutory parish meeting may—

(a) if there is a vestry for that worship centre, resolve not to have a vestry for that worship centre; and

(b) if there is no vestry for that worship centre or it has resolved not to have a vestry for that worship centre, resolve that there is not in future to be an annual meeting for that worship centre.

(4) A local statutory parish meeting of a local worship centre that has no vestry and no annual meeting may resolve that this section no longer applies.

(5) This section no longer applies if a local statutory parish meeting of every local worship centre that has previously resolved that this section applies has resolved that this section no longer applies.

19. Disqualification from holding parish offices

(1) Subject to sub-section (3) a person who is—

(a) an undischarged bankrupt; or

(b) a person who has been convicted of an offence punishable by more than 5 years imprisonment; or

(c) permanently or for a period of more than 12 months incapable to a substantial degree by reason of mental incapacity or physical disability to discharge the duties of a parish office—

is a disqualified person and may not be a parish officer.

(2) A person who is subject to a prohibition order under the *Professional Standards Act 2009* may not be a parish officer in relation to any position, office or function which they are prohibited from holding or carrying out under that Act, and that person is a disqualified person to the extent, but only to the extent, of that prohibition.

(3) The Archbishop, on the advice of the Chancellor, may exempt a person in whole or in part from the application of sub-section (1).

(4) The participation of a disqualified person in a meeting of a parish does not invalidate the meeting or any proceedings at it.

20. Declaration by office holders

(1) Subject to sub-section (2), a person appointed or elected to a parish office must not perform any duties of that office before signing a declaration in or to the effect of the prescribed form.

(2) Sub-section (1) applies to a person not already a member of the parish council appointed temporarily to act as a churchwarden or treasurer, but not to a person so appointed who is at the time of the appointment already a member of the parish council or to a member of an incumbency committee referred to in section 21(1)(b).

(3) If a person fails to comply with sub-section (1) within one month of being appointed or elected, the office becomes vacant.

21. Incumbency committee

(1) The incumbency committee of a parish comprises—

    (a) subject to this section, the Regional Bishop of the Region in which the parish lies, who chairs the committee;

    (b) a churchwarden appointed in accordance with sub-sections (2), (3) or (3A);

    (c) the parishioners elected in accordance with sub-sections (4) or (5) or filling a vacancy in the position of a parishioner so elected;

    (d) the local archdeacon; and

    (e) the consultant appointed to the incumbency committee in accordance with section 17 of the *Appointments Act 1971*.

(2) Within 30 days of an annual meeting or before the first meeting of the parish council following an annual meeting (whichever occurs first), the churchwardens must appoint a churchwarden to be a member of the incumbency committee.

(3) If the person appointed under sub-section (2) is for any reason no longer available at the time when the incumbency committee is first convened, the churchwardens must, before the first meeting of the incumbency committee, appoint to the incumbency committee a churchwarden who is not a member of the incumbency committee elected under sub-section (4).

(3A) If after an incumbency committee has first met a churchwarden appointed to it under sub-sections (2) or (3) or this sub-section ceases to be a churchwarden, the churchwardens must within 30 days appoint to the incumbency committee a churchwarden who is not a member of the incumbency committee elected under sub-section (4). If that person is on an incumbency committee reserve list, the person ceases to be on that reserve list at the time of being appointed under this sub-section.

(4) Other than the churchwarden appointed in accordance with sub-sections (2), (3) or (3A), the parishioners who are members of the incumbency committee are—
   (a) where there is one worship centre, two parishioners elected by the annual meeting; and
   (b) where there is more than one worship centre, one parishioner elected by the parish annual meeting plus one parishioner on the local electoral roll of each worship centre in the parish, elected by the parishioners on that local electoral roll.
   Note: The election of parishioners on local electoral rolls could take place at the time of the annual meeting of the parish.

(4A) At the time of electing parishioners under sub-section (4), a meeting may also elect parishioners to a list to be known as the incumbency committee reserve list.

(4B) An incumbency committee reserve list elected by a meeting of a parish or worship centre is a reserve list solely in respect of those parishioners elected as members of the incumbency committee by a meeting of that same parish or worship centre.

(5) If there is a vacancy in the elected parishioners on the incumbency committee before its first meeting, the vacancy may be filled—
   (a) in the case of a parishioner elected by an annual meeting or a parish electoral meeting, by a special parish electoral meeting; and

(b) in other cases, by a special meeting of the parishioners on the relevant local electoral roll.

(5A) If at a meeting under sub-section (5)—

(a) a parishioner on the incumbency committee reserve list is elected to the incumbency committee; or

(b) there is a vacancy on the incumbency committee reserve list arising from the appointment under sub-sections (2) or (3) of a parishioner elected to that list—

the meeting may fill any vacancy on the incumbency committee reserve list that it is entitled to fill by an election conducted following a call for nominations from the floor of the meeting.

(5B) If there is a vacancy in the elected parishioners on the incumbency committee and—

(a) the vacancy has not been filled under sub-section (5); or

(b) the vacancy occurs after the incumbency committee has met—

the vacancy may be filled from the relevant incumbency committee reserve list. Where there is more than one person on an incumbency committee reserve list, the order in which those persons are to fill vacancies on the incumbency committee is to be determined by agreement between them or, in the absence of agreement, by lot.

(6) As soon as possible after a parishioner becomes a member of the incumbency committee, the parish must inform the Registrar of his or her name and postal address.

(6A) After the first meeting of an incumbency committee, the lay members of the committee elected or appointed under this section continue as members until the institution of the next vicar, and any persons elected or appointed under this section (other than under sub-sections (3A) or (5B)) after the first meeting of an incumbency meeting are elected or appointed only for the purposes of being members of an incumbency committee convened after the institution of the next vicar.

(7) The Archbishop may determine that he or she, or another person whom he or she appoints for the purpose, is to be a member of and is to chair the committee instead of the Regional Bishop.

22. Status of decisions

(1) The parish council must take into consideration any expression of opinion by a statutory parish meeting.

(2) Except as otherwise provided by this or any other Act, a decision of a statutory parish meeting is not binding on the parish council or churchwardens unless it is a decision requiring that a matter be considered or taken into account, or a decision seeking a report in relation to a matter.

(3) A decision of a parish council is not binding on the churchwardens in relation to any matter for which they have a statutory responsibility.

PART 5—RESPONSIBILITIES IN PARISH GOVERNANCE

Division 1—The churchwardens and parish council

23. Churchwardens

(1) Subject to this Act, the churchwardens of a parish are responsible for—

   (a) the care and maintenance of the church, the vicarage and other accommodation provided by the parish for the staff of the parish, the church grounds, and all other buildings and property of the parish;

(b) the care of the furniture of the worship centres and of all things necessary for the conduct of public worship, and for providing everything necessary for the conduct of public worship, including the bread and wine for the Holy Communion;

(c) keeping in order the worship centres and their grounds and seeing that everything in and about the worship centres is fit and in proper order for the due performance of public worship;

(d) keeping order in the worship centres during public worship and providing for the due seating of the congregation and the collection of their offerings;

(e) reporting to the parish council all repairs or alterations required in the fabric, fittings or furniture of the worship centres and the fabric and fittings of the vicarage;

(f) complying with any laws of the Commonwealth of Australia, the State of Victoria or any municipality in which the parish has property that impose mandatory requirements applicable to the land, buildings and operations of the parish; and

(g) the other functions and responsibilities imposed on them by this Act.

(2) The churchwardens must ensure that any leave taken by the vicar is consistent with the terms of the vicar's appointment.

(3) Except where the churchwardens have a duty to report the matter under section 22 of the *Professional Standards Act 2009*, the churchwardens of the parish have a duty to provide a written report to the Archbishop, signed by a majority of them, on any serious irregularities in the

performance of public worship or any wilful neglect of duty or any serious misconduct on the part of the vicar.

(4) The churchwardens have the functions and duties conferred or imposed by the laws of the Church, including canons of General Synod adopted by this Diocese and the laws of this Diocese.

24. Role of the vicar

The vicar has a distinct role in governance and management of the parish and—

(a) is responsible for the administration of public worship, for the preaching and teaching of the word of God, for the administration of the sacraments, and for its whole mission, pastoral, evangelistic, social, and ecumenical;

(b) contributes biblical, theological, pastoral, liturgical, educational, evangelistic and ethical insights to the governance and management of the parish;

(c) works in cooperation with the churchwardens and parish council in ensuring that the governance and management of the parish serves the identity and whole mission of the church;

(d) exercises a presidential role by chairing the parish council, the vestry and statutory parish meetings, or by appointing other fit persons to chair such meetings as provided for by this Act and the parish rules for meetings and officers, and is entitled to exercise a vote at a meeting of the parish council or a vestry (whether chairing the meeting or not), but is not entitled to exercise a vote at statutory parish meetings;

(e) may make appointments jointly with the churchwardens under the Act; and

(f) may recommend to the Archbishop persons to be appointed

to ministry in the parish as a clerk or as an authorised lay minister.

25. Functions of the parish council

(1) The functions of the parish council include, in addition to the functions contained in this or any other Act—

    (a) promoting in the parish the whole mission of the Church, pastoral, evangelistic, social and ecumenical;

    (b) supporting and assisting the churchwardens in the discharge of their responsibilities;

    (c) the consideration and discussion of matters concerning the Anglican Church or any other matters of religious or public interest but not the declaration of the doctrine of the Anglican Church on any question;

    (d) making known and putting into effect any provision made by the Diocesan Synod;

    (e) giving advice to the Diocesan Synod on any matter referred to the parish council; and

    (f) raising such matters as the parish council considers appropriate with the Diocesan Synod.

(2) The parish council must consult together on matters of general concern and importance to the parish.

(3) The parish council must have in place and review annually a plan setting out material risks and the mitigation strategies.

Division 2—Appointments

26. Interpretation

In this Division, a reference to authorised lay ministry is a reference to lay ministry of a kind that is or may be authorised pursuant to the Authorised Lay Ministry Canon 1992 of the General Synod of the Anglican Church, and a reference to authorised lay minister is a reference to a person authorised for authorised lay ministry.

27. Appointments generally

(1) The parish council may determine amounts to be available for the remuneration of the holders of any role, office or position in the parish and, subject to the *Diocesan Stipends Act 1991*, must determine the remuneration payable in each case.

(2) A person appointed to a role, office or position in a parish must be fit to hold the role, office or position in the Anglican Church whether unconditionally or subject to any condition or restriction.

(3) A person appointed to hold any role, office or position in a parish for ordained ministry or for authorised lay ministry must not engage in that ministry without the licence or other written authority of the Archbishop which shall be conclusive evidence of their fitness for that role, office or position.

(4) Except with the prior written consent of the relevant Archdeacon (or, in a parish in which the Archdeacon is the incumbent, the Archbishop or the relevant Regional Bishop), a churchwarden may not be appointed to, or continue to hold, a remunerated office or position in the parish.

28. Appointments of clerks and authorised lay ministers

(1) The Archbishop alone may appoint—
   (a) a person in Holy Orders to a stipendiary role, office or position in a parish; and
   (b) a stipendiary authorised lay minister in a parish—
   and alone may suspend or terminate that appointment.

(2) An appointment under sub-section (1) is on the terms and conditions determined by the Archbishop.

(3) The vicar is responsible for recommending to the Archbishop the appointment of a person under sub-section (1) and the terms and conditions of that appointment.

(4) The Archbishop must consult with the vicar before exercising the power of appointment, suspension or termination unless it is impracticable to do so.

(5) The vicar is responsible for supervising and managing a person appointed under this section.

(6) Nothing in this section applies to the appointment of a person as the vicar or derogates from the inherent powers or authority of the Archbishop.

29. Other appointments

(1) Except as provided in sub-section (4) of this section and otherwise in this Act, the vicar alone may appoint on such terms and conditions as he or she determines a person to any role, office or position in the parish and alone may suspend or terminate that appointment.

(2) The vicar may authorize a person on his or her behalf to manage and supervise a person appointed under sub-section (1).

(3) The vicar may delegate to the relevant Archdeacon or to another person approved by the Archbishop his or her duties and functions as the Church authority under the *Professional Standards Act 2009* in relation to a person appointed under sub-section (1).

(4) Except as otherwise provided in this Act or in the parish rules for meetings and officers, the vicar and churchwardens may jointly appoint on such terms and conditions as they determine—

    (a) a person to any remunerated role, office or position

in the parish that is not in relation to public worship, mission, ministry or teaching; and

(b) a person to any role, office or position in the parish involving the handling or collection of moneys or the keeping of parish books and records—

and may jointly suspend or terminate that appointment.

(5) The vicar and churchwardens may jointly authorize one of their number on their behalf to manage and supervise the person in the role, office or position.

(6) The vicar and the churchwardens may jointly delegate to one of their number or to the relevant Archdeacon or to another person approved by the Archbishop their duties and functions as the Church authority under the *Professional Standards Act 2009* in relation to a person appointed under sub-section (4).

Division 3—Annual diocesan assessment

30. *Annual diocesan assessments*

(1) A parish must pay from its funds to the Diocese in accordance with this section the annual diocesan assessment specified in sub-section (5) or as otherwise determined under section 31.

(2) The annual diocesan assessment is to be applied for the purpose of contributing to—

(a) funds recognized by the Archbishop in Council as being required by the Diocesan Corporation for its purposes;

(aa) funds to be expended by the Archbishop in Council or in accordance with the budget of the Archbishop in Council;

(b) the expenses of the Synod;

       (c)   funds authorized or required to be expended by statute or resolution of Synod, and

       (d)   purposes incidental to any of the foregoing items of expenditure.

(3)   The assessment is an amount determined in the manner prescribed by the Archbishop in Council on the basis of the annual income of the parish, net of allowable deductions and at a stipulated rate of assessment.

(4)   For the purpose of determining the annual diocesan assessment, the parish must give the Registrar an annual statement of the income and expenditure of the parish in the form and at the time prescribed.

(5)   The Registrar must determine the annual diocesan assessment in the manner prescribed and issue a notice of assessment to the parish.

(6)   The parish must discharge its obligations under this Part within the time and in the manner prescribed.

31. Objection to annual diocesan assessment

(1)   A parish may within a prescribed time in the prescribed form object to the Archbishop in Council against the annual diocesan assessment.

(2)   The grounds for the objection must be stated fully and in detail, and must be in writing.

(3)   The Archbishop in Council may following an objection under sub-section (1), allow the objection and determine an annual diocesan assessment in lieu of the annual diocesan assessment determined by the Registrar under section 30(5).

32. Waiver of annual diocesan assessment

(1)   A parish may within a prescribed time apply to the Archbishop in Council for some or all of its obligation to pay the annual diocesan assessment to be waived.

(2) The Archbishop in Council may at the time when a parish is first created or following an application under sub-section (1), in its absolute discretion waive in whole or in part a parish's obligation to pay the annual diocesan assessment on such terms and conduct as it may decide.

(3) The Archbishop in Council must adopt and publish a policy guiding the exercise of its discretion under sub-section (2).

Division 4—Finance

33. Parish council and parish budget

(1) The parish council has the general direction of the administration of all parish funds other than those excluded from that direction by the trusts on which they are held, and must provide that direction in accordance with this Division.

(2) The parish council must approve and present to each annual meeting a parish budget for the financial year in which the meeting is held.

(3) The parish budget must specify an amount with regard to each of the matters for which payment must be made under section 35(1).

(4) The parish council may alter the parish budget to respond to unforeseen increases or decreases in income, expenditure, assets or liabilities.

(5) The treasurer must ensure that the funds of the parish are expended in a manner consistent with the parish budget.

(6) In this Division, **parish budget** means the parish budget approved and presented under sub-section (2) as altered under sub-section (4).

34. Parish funds

(1) The churchwardens have responsibility for the proper keeping and management of all parish funds and must

maintain adequate and accurate accounting records of the parish's financial transactions.

(2) The funds of the parish must be kept in an account in the name of the parish with a bank or with some other prescribed institution.

(3) Subject to this section—
    (a) the signatories for payments from the funds of the parish are the treasurer, the churchwardens and any other persons decided by the parish council; and
    (b) a cheque or other payment from the funds of the parish must be signed or authorized by two signatories, one of whom is the treasurer or a churchwarden.

(4) All money received by the parish in order for it to be remitted to a person or body outside the parish must be paid to that person or body within two months of its being received.

(5) A person must not incur a liability on behalf of the parish except as authorized by the parish council.

(6) The parish council must establish a proper system for monitoring the incurring of liabilities on behalf of the parish to ensure that liabilities are incurred within the scope and terms of the authorization.

(7) The Archbishop in Council may make regulations regarding the systems to be established under sub-section (6).

35. *Application of parish funds*

(1) The parish must out of its funds pay for—
    (a) the supply of all things necessary for public worship and the administration of the sacraments;
    (b) the amounts of remuneration determined under section 27(1);
    (c) the insurance required by section 39;

(d) the payment of interest on money borrowed for the erection of the worship centre, vicarage or other parish buildings; and

(e) the annual diocesan assessment.

(2) If any rent is received for the buildings of the parish, the insurance and repairs of those buildings must be met first from the rent.

(3) After making due provision for any existing debt, the parish budget may provide for—

(a) the investment of any surplus funds in the manner prescribed;

(b) the expenditure of surplus funds for such pious and charitable uses as the parish council may think fit; or

(c) retaining surplus funds in an operating account of the parish.

36. Other provisions relating to management of parish funds

(1) Despite any other provision of this Act—

(a) money raised by or contributed to the parish in connection with the parish church or other parochial buildings or for improving or furnishing them, or for any other purpose or purposes connected with the Anglican Church or any of its schools, societies, clubs, committees or other institution; and

(b) money raised or contributed to the parish from any trust or corporation established for the benefit of the parish or to advance any mission or ministry for which the parish is responsible—

must be shown in the accounts of the parish.

(2) The vicar, other than in the discharge of the responsibilities provided for in this Act, must not have any involvement in the management or administration of the finances or

financial arrangements other than as a member of the parish council or a sub-committee of the parish council.

Division 5—Property held for parish purposes

37. Use of property held by a parish for parish purposes

(1) The parish council must ensure that the uses to which property held or controlled for parish purposes are put are consistent with the fundamental beliefs and principles of the Christian church and the good name and repute of the Anglican Church.

(2) A meeting (other than a duly called statutory parish meeting or a meeting of a parish council or vestry) may not be held in any parochial building (including a worship centre) without the consent of the vicar.

(3) The fittings and furniture of a new church may be installed, and the fabric, fittings and furniture of any church may be added to, altered or removed, only by the churchwardens with the approval of the vicar and parish council and the written consent of the Archbishop.

(4) A monument must not be placed within or on the walls of a church without a faculty from the Archbishop.

(5) The churchwardens must not remove or reinstate anything installed, added, altered or removed otherwise than in accordance with this section or without any necessary faculty.

(6) This section does not prevent the churchwardens from repairing and maintaining the fabric, fittings and furniture of a church as closely as possible to their original condition.

(7) In this section, "fittings" includes monuments, stained glass windows and any fixtures primarily ornamental or

decorative affixed to or incorporated into the fabric of the church.

(8) The churchwardens, with the consent of the vicar and parish council, may permit any monument to be placed in any part of a church or church grounds upon payment of such charges and subject to such regulations as are prescribed and the person so placing a monument, and the person's heirs, administrators and executors, may maintain and keep up the monument to and for his, her or their sole and separate use.

38. Property rights of the incumbent and vicar

(1) The vicar is entitled to the means of access (including keys, security passes and security codes) to all the worship centres and other buildings of the parish used for parish purposes, and is to have unimpeded access at all times to the worship centres and those other buildings.

(2) The vicar is entitled to lead public worship, administer the sacraments and perform all other rites and ordinances of the Anglican Church without hindrance from any one.

(3) The incumbent is entitled to reside in the vicarage and, when resident, to the free and unimpeded use and enjoyment of the vicarage and any land associated with it.

(4) The vicar may not let or otherwise part with possession of the vicarage, and if the incumbent does not reside in the vicarage the parish council is responsible for deciding how it and any land associated with it are to be occupied or otherwise used.

(5) The incumbent must not, without the prior consent in writing of the Archbishop following consultation with the parish council, reside beyond the boundaries of the parish.

(6) The rights and entitlements of an incumbent continue only for as long as he or she is the incumbent.

39. Parish insurance

(1) A parish must maintain adequate insurance for—
   (a) all the buildings of the parish;
   (b) the contents of all the buildings of the parish;
   (c) loss or damage occurring in connection with the ownership, management, control or use of the buildings of the parish and their contents and of the grounds of the parish; and
   (d) any liability of the parish officers incurred in that capacity (including any legal fees, fines or penalties) other than as a result of their fraud or wilful misconduct.

(2) Sub-section (1) does not require a parish to insure against any loss or damage against which the Diocesan Trusts Corporation has insured in accordance with the *Diocese of Melbourne Insurance Act 1986*.

(3) The parish must pay the insurance premiums that are from time to time determined under the *Diocese of Melbourne Insurance Act 1986* by the Archbishop in Council to be payable by the parish to the Diocesan Trusts Corporation or any other body.

(4) The churchwardens must maintain a full and complete inventory of all registers, records, legal documents and of all furniture, service books, and vessels belonging to the parish and must provide to the Registrar a copy of the inventory as it is updated from time to time.

40. Public worship

(1) Except with the prior written authorization of the Archbishop, the vicar and the churchwardens, a worship centre must not be used for any purpose other than public worship, the administration of the sacraments, the

performance of the rites and ordinances of the Anglican Church or religious instruction or devotion.

(2) Public worship must be conducted in accordance with—
  (a) a form of service contained in:
    (i) the Book of Common Prayer;
    (ii) An Australian Prayer Book;
    (iii) A Prayer Book for Australia; or
  (b) deviations from any of those forms permitted by the Archbishop under section 4 of the Constitution of the Anglican Church; or
  (c) variations to any of those forms which are not of substantial importance according to particular circumstances and which are authorized under a Canon of the Anglican Church adopted by the Diocese.

(3) Subject to sub-section (4), a person other than the Archbishop or the relevant Regional Bishop may not perform a clerical office in a worship centre without the consent of the vicar and the Archbishop.

(4) A clerk in holy orders authorized to officiate in the Diocese may perform a clerical office in a worship centre with the consent of the vicar alone or, if the vicar is suspended from office or for any other reason not capable of consenting, with the consent of the Archbishop.

(5) The time or mode of conducting the principal service in a worship centre may be changed only with the consent of the vicar and the parish council given at a meeting summoned for the purpose and ratified at another meeting not more than six months later.

Division 6—Preparation, audit and independent examination of accounts

41. *Statements of money raised for parish*

(1) A treasurer or other person who has the custody or control of any money of the parish must each year, at least 14 days before the date of the annual meeting and at other times when called upon by the churchwardens, provide to the churchwardens a statement of accounts and balance sheet.

(2) The churchwardens must to the fullest extent that it is possible for them to do so obtain the most recent profit and loss statement and balance sheet of every trust or corporation established—
   (a) for the benefit of the parish; or
   (b) to advance any mission or ministry for which the parish is responsible—
and of which the vicar or any parish officer is an officer.

42. *Churchwardens to prepare accounts*

(1) As soon as possible after the end of a financial year the churchwardens must prepare the accounts in respect of that financial year to be tabled at the annual meeting.

(2) The accounts must be prepared in accordance with the following principles—
   (a) there must be an abstract of accounts of all moneys received and expended during the financial year that gives a true and fair view of the incoming resources and the application of the resources in that financial year;
   (b) there must be a statement of all assets and liabilities of and in connection with the parish as at the end of the financial year that gives a true and fair view of the state of affairs of the parish at the end of that financial year.

(3) The notes in Schedule 3 must be provided with the accounts to the extent necessary to show a true and fair view of the accounts.

(4) The churchwardens must—
- (a) show the accounts to the parish council before the annual meeting;
- (b) submit the accounts to the auditors or the independent examiner together with all accounting records required by the auditors or the independent examiner;
- (c) have the accounts, the certificate of the auditors or the independent examiner, and the statements and balance sheets obtained by them under section 41(2) printed and made available in printed form to the parishioners attending the annual meeting; and
- (d) send to the Registrar within seven days after the annual meeting two copies of the documents printed for the annual meeting.

(5) The churchwardens must—
- (a) inform the annual meeting of any material change, as at the date of the meeting, in the income, expenditure, assets or liabilities from that shown in the accounts and the budget presented to the meeting; and
- (b) immediately after the annual meeting, give to their successors, all accounting records and other documents relevant to the financial administration of the parish.

43. Audit and independent examination

(1) The annual meeting of a parish whose total receipts in the financial year immediately preceding that annual meeting exceed $250,000 must appoint an auditor.

(2) The annual meeting of a parish to which sub-section (1) does not apply must appoint either—
- (a) an auditor; or
- (b) an independent examiner.

(3) If at any time a position of auditor or independent examiner

becomes vacant, the parish council must appoint an auditor or independent examiner to fill the vacancy.

(4) An auditor or independent examiner appointed under this section holds office until the next annual meeting unless in the meantime the auditor or independent examiner—

(a) dies;

(b) resigns; or

(c) is removed by resolution of a special meeting.

44. Qualifications of auditor

An auditor must be—

(a) a registered company auditor under the Corporations Act 2001 (Cth);

(b) a firm of registered company auditors under the Corporations Act 2001 (Cth);

(c) a person who is a member of CPA Australia or the Institute of Chartered Accountants in Australia; or

(d) a person who is approved by the Registrar of Incorporated Associations under section 99(5) of the *Associations Incorporation Reform Act 2012* of the State of Victoria to audit financial statements.

45. Duties of the auditor

(1) The auditor must —

(a) audit or review the accounts in accordance with this Act and the Australian Auditing Standards made by the Auditing and Assurance Standards Board under the Corporations Act 2001 (Cth); and

(b) report to the Registrar as soon as practicable in the prescribed form if a matter of material significance has arisen.

(2) The auditor must give to the churchwardens before the

annual meeting a report on the results of the audit or review (as the case may be) which—

(a) states his or her name and address and the name of the parish;

(b) is signed by him or her and specifies any relevant qualifications or professional body of which he or she is a member;

(c) is dated and specifies the financial year in respect of which the accounts to which it relates have been prepared;

(d) specifies that it is a report in respect of an audit or review carried out under section 45 of the Act;

(e) in the case of an audit, states whether in the auditor's opinion:

   (i) the accounts comply with the requirements of section 42 of the Act; and

   (ii) the accounts give a true and fair view of the moneys received and expended and of the state of affairs of the parish at the end of the financial year in question;

(f) in the case of a review, reports as a matter of fact whether on the basis of the review assignment, anything has come to the auditor's attention that causes the auditor to believe that the financial report is not prepared in accordance with the requirements of section 42(2);

(g) states whether or not any matter has come to the auditor's attention, in connection with the audit or review, which gives him or her reasonable cause to believe that in any material respect:

   (i) accounting records have not been kept in

respect of the parish in accordance with this Act; or

    (ii)   the accounts do not accord with those records;

(h)   states whether or not any matter has come to the auditor's attention in connection with the audit or review to which, in his or her opinion, attention should be drawn in the accounts in order to enable a proper understanding of the accounts to be reached; and

(i)   contains a statement as to any of the following matters that has become apparent to the auditor during the course of the audit or review:

    (i)   that a matter of material significance has arisen;

    (ii)   that any information or explanation to which the auditor is entitled under this Act has not been made available to him or her.

46. Qualifications of independent examiner

The independent examiner must be an independent person who is nominated by the churchwardens and whom they reasonably believe has the requisite ability and practical experience to carry out a competent examination of the accounts.

47. Duties of independent examiner

(1)   The independent examiner must—

    (a)   undertake an independent examination of the accounts in accordance with this Act and any procedures prescribed by Archbishop in Council; and

    (b)   report to the Registrar and the churchwardens as soon as practicable in a form prescribed if a matter of material significance has arisen.

(2)   The independent examiner must give the churchwardens prior to the annual meeting a report on the results of the independent examination which—

(a) states his or her name and address and the name of the parish;

(b) is signed by him or her and specifies any relevant qualifications or professional body of which he or she is a member;

(c) is dated and specifies the financial year in respect of which the accounts to which it relates have been prepared;

(d) specifies that it is a report in respect of an examination carried out under section 47 of the Act;

(e) states whether or not any matter has come to the independent examiner's attention, in connection with the examination, which gives him or her reasonable cause to believe that in any material respect:

    (i) accounting records have not been kept in respect of the parish in accordance with the Act; or

    (ii) the accounts do not accord with those records; or

    (iii) the accounts do not comply with any of the requirements of section 42(2), other than any requirement to give a true and fair view;

(f) states whether or not any matter has come to the independent examiner's attention in connection with the examination to which, in his or her opinion, attention should be drawn in the accounts in order to enable a proper understanding of the accounts to be reached;

(g) contains a statement as to any of the following matters that has become apparent to the independent examiner during the course of the examination:

    (i) that a matter of material significance has arisen;

    (ii) that any information or explanation to which the independent examiner is entitled under this Act has not been made available to him or her.

48. Access and information

 (1) An auditor or independent examiner carrying out an audit, review or examination has a right of access to any books, documents and other records (however kept) which relate to the parish and which the auditor or independent examiner considers it necessary to inspect for the purpose of carrying out the audit, review or examination.

 (2) An auditor or independent examiner may require such information and explanations from past or present parish officers or clergy of the parish as he or she considers it necessary to obtain for the purposes of carrying out the audit, review or examination.

49. Meaning of material significance

For the purposes of this Division, a matter of material significance will have arisen if the person is aware of circumstances that the person has reasonable grounds to suspect may amount to—

 (a) a failure in a significant respect of any of the treasurer, the churchwardens or the parish council to comply with a provision of this Act;

 (b) dishonesty or fraud involving a loss of parish funds or a risk of loss of parish funds; or

 (c) a breach in a significant respect of the terms of any special trust to which property enjoyed by the parish is subject.

50. Accounts to be dealt with by annual meeting

 (1) The annual meeting may receive and adopt the accounts or may refer them back to the churchwardens and auditors or the independent examiner for further report and

information and may adjourn the annual meeting for the purpose of considering them further.

(2) Despite any other provision in this Act or in a rule for meetings and officers, if the churchwardens do not as required by section 42(4)(c) at the annual meeting of a parish have the accounts and the certificate of the auditors or the independent examiner printed and made available in printed form to the parishioners attending that annual meeting, the person chairing that meeting must, when all the other business of the meeting has been concluded, adjourn the meeting to a date not later than the end of February next following, for the purpose of considering at that meeting so adjourned the accounts so certified.

51. *Registrar's request for further information*

(1) The Registrar may refer the accounts back to the churchwardens and the auditors or independent examiner for further information.

(2) If the accounts are referred back under this section, the churchwardens and the auditors or independent examiner who were in office at the time of the previous annual meeting must supply the information.

52. *Audit by Registrar*

If it appears to the Registrar on reasonable grounds that the churchwardens or the auditors or independent examiner have not complied with section 42(4) or section 51 the Registrar may cause an audit to be undertaken of the accounts for that year.

Division 7—Registers, records and other documents

53. *Registers and records*

(1) The vicar must keep or cause to be kept and have the custody and control of the registers and records relating to—

(a) baptisms;
(b) persons prepared and presented for confirmation;
(c) marriages solemnised;
(d) funerals, memorial services, burials and interments of ashes;
(e) public worship.

(2) The registers and records must be in the prescribed form and clearly show the prescribed particulars.

(3) The churchwardens must provide the vicar with the necessary books and with a safe place to store them.

(4) The registers and records are the property of the parish and not of the vicar by whom they were compiled.

(5) At the end of an incumbency or when the incumbent is suspended, he or she must surrender all the registers and records under his or her control to the churchwardens, who must give the incumbent a written receipt for them.

(6) The churchwardens must hand to an incoming incumbent the registers and records of the parish and the incumbent must give the churchwardens a written receipt for them.

54. Inspecting the condition of books and records

(1) The Archdeacon or Area Dean may inspect any books, registers, records or legal documents of a parish and report on their condition if required by the Archbishop to do so.

(2) Any information in a register or record of an act of public worship is open to public inspection if that information was available to a person attending that act of public worship.

Division 8—Periodic parish reviews

55. Periodic review

(1) A parish may with the consent of the parish council and the agreement of the Archbishop on the recommendation

of the Registrar and the relevant Archdeacon (or, in the case of a parish the incumbent of which is the Archdeacon, the relevant Regional Bishop) conduct a periodic review in accordance with this section.

(2) The purpose of a periodic review is to generate information based on common criteria regarding the health and potential for the church in the diocese, and to assist the Archbishop in Council, Archdeacons and the parish itself in understanding and planning for the future. The scope of the review must include the effectiveness of the governance of the parish.

(3) The parish council must collect the data prescribed by Archbishop in Council for use in all periodic reviews of parishes. The data may include statistical and quantitative data, and information gathered from parish officers and parishioners.

(4) The data is to be assessed by an external reviewer and made the basis of a report to the parish and to the Regional Bishop.

(5) Within three months of the completion of the report, the report must be presented to and discussed at a special meeting of the parish called for the purpose which is chaired by the Archdeacon (or, in the case of a parish of which the Archdeacon is the vicar, the Regional Bishop or some other Archdeacon nominated by the Archbishop or the Regional Bishop) and at which the external reviewer is present and able to speak.

(6) The external reviewer is a person appointed by the Registrar after consultation with the Archdeacon (or, in the case of a parish of which the Archdeacon is the vicar, with the

Archbishop or the Regional Bishop) from a panel approved by the Archbishop in Council.

PART 6—PARISH CO-OPERATION

Division 1—Introduction

56. Possible co-operative arrangements

(1) Two or more parishes may enter into co-operative arrangements in accordance with this Part.

(2) Division 2 is concerned with co-operative arrangements that involve the sharing of property, ministry or governance.

(3) Division 3 is concerned with co-operative arrangements that involve the use of shared resources.

Division 2—Shared property, ministry or governance

57. Co-operative agreement

(1) Two or more parishes may enter into an arrangement by which, while retaining their legal status as parishes, they share responsibility for and access to one or more of ministry, mission and property, and put in place the joint governance to the necessary extent.

(2) Before an arrangement is entered into a statutory parish meeting of each parish and the Archbishop in Council must approve a written agreement, to be signed by the churchwardens of each parish, that sets out, insofar as any of these matters is within the scope of a parish and subject to sub-section (3)—

   (a) the motivation for the parish;
   (b) the outcomes sought from the parish;
   (c) how it will be evaluated;

(d) the specific arrangements and agreed expectations regarding:
    (i) governance and leadership roles;
    (ii) voting rights and election processes;
    (iii) the shared use of, and access to, property;
    (iv) the application of income derived from the use of property;
    (v) the maintenance of property and any associated costs;
    (vi) responsibility for insurance and risk management in relation to shared resources;
    (vii) making appointments and the supervision of staff and contractors;
    (viii) financial arrangements;
    (ix) reporting and the sharing of information;
    (x) the times and mode of public worship services;
    (xi) licensed ministry and other clergy, including how they are to be appointed, supervised, evaluated and replaced;
    (xii) appointing, supervising, evaluating and replacing other paid and unpaid staff.
    (xiii) what is to happen if one parish fails to adhere to the agreement;
    (xiv) how disputes are to be resolved;
    (xv) how the arrangement is to be reviewed and can be terminated;

(e) a provision that the agreement is terminated automatically on the expiration of 10 years from the date it was last made unless it is renewed with the consent of a statutory parish meeting of each parish and the Archbishop in Council.

(3) A term in an agreement that alters or modifies the operation of this Act or any other Diocesan legislation as it applies to one or more of the parishes who are parties to it has effect only if the term is set out in a schedule separately approved by the Archbishop in Council.

(4) Once approved and in place, an agreement must be lodged with the Diocesan registry.

58. Ministry areas

(1) A co-operative agreement under section 57 may provide that the parishes come together as a ministry area.

(2) A co-operative agreement to establish a ministry area, in addition to satisfying the requirements of section 57—

(a) may provide for a ministry team in the parish or parishes concerned that includes chaplains and other persons licensed by the Archbishop to special ministries within those parishes;

(b) may provide for a priest to be designated by the Archbishop to be the leader of ministry within the ministry area, while maintaining the rights and responsibilities of any vicar in any of the parishes concerned;

(c) may provide for a priest who is the leader of ministry to share in the oversight of the parish congregations in the ministry area with the Archbishop, the Regional Bishop and each vicar in that ministry area;

(d) may provide that the responsibilities of the members of the ministry team would be those agreed amongst the Regional Bishop (or, if the Archbishop so determines, the Archbishop), the members of the ministry team and each parish council concerned; and

(e) may provide for a ministry area constitution that establishes a ministry area council.

59. Licensing of a clerk to more than one parish

(1) Despite any law, rule or practice of the church to the contrary (other than a law of the Anglican Church of Australia), but subject to this section, where there is in place a co-operative arrangement between parishes in accordance with this Division, the Archbishop may license or appoint a clerk to be the vicar in more than one of those parishes.

(2) A clerk licensed or appointed as the vicar in more than one parish is entitled to a stipend only in respect of one of those parishes.

Division 3—Shared resources

60. Arrangements for the sharing of resources

(1) Two or more parishes may enter into an arrangement for jointly sourcing goods or services or for cooperative activity in the ministry and mission of the church.

(2) An arrangement referred to in sub-section (1) must be set out in a written agreement, approved by the parish council of each parish concerned and by the Archbishop in Council and signed by the churchwardens of each parish concerned, covering—

(a) the motivation for the parish and the outcomes sought;

(b) how the arrangement will be evaluated;

(c) the specific arrangements and agreed expectations regarding:

(i) governance and leadership roles;

(ii) financial arrangements, including how profits and losses are to be allocated;

(iii) responsibility for insurance and risk management in relation to shared resources;

                (iv)   appointing and supervising service providers;
                (v)   reporting and the sharing of information;
                (vi)   what is to happen if a parish fails to adhere to the agreement;
                (vii)   how disputes are to be resolved;
                (viii) how the arrangement is to be reviewed and can be terminated;
        (d)   the automatic termination of the agreement on the expiration of five years from the date it was last made unless it is renewed by the churchwardens of the parishes concerned.
(3)   A term in an agreement that alters or modifies the operation of this Act or any other Diocesan legislation as it applies to one or more of the parishes who are parties to it has effect only if the term is set out in a schedule separately approved by the Archbishop in Council.
(4)   An agreement under this section must be lodged with the Diocesan registry.

PART 7—SPECIAL CIRCUMSTANCES

Division 1—Supported parishes

61. *Designation as a supported parish*

(1)   Where the Archbishop in Council considers that—
        (a)   it is necessary for the advancement of the church that a parish be established or retained in a particular geographic area; and
        (b)   it is unrealistic to expect that the resources required to maintain a viable parish and to discharge the functions and responsibilities imposed by this Act and by other laws can be found within that parish

it may designate the parish a supported parish.

(2) Except where a parish is designated a supported parish at the time when it is established under section 6 or the Archbishop in Council is acting in accordance with a provision in Division 3 of Part 7, before a parish is designated a supported parish the Archbishop in Council must consult the vicar and the parish council and a statutory parish meeting must agree to the designation.

(3) In relation to a supported parish, by written agreement to which the parties are the Archbishop, the relevant Regional Bishop or the relevant Archdeacon, the Registrar and the churchwardens of the parish—

   (a) the Registrar may assume any or all of the responsibilities of the parish council, churchwardens, treasurer or parish secretary contained in this Act or the parish rules for meetings and officers; and

   (b) the requirements of this and any other Diocesan legislation in relation to meetings and elections may be altered, while preserving as far as possible the right of parishioners to participate in making decisions relating to the life of the parish.

(4) Despite anything in any other legislation, with effect from the date of the next mandate given by the Archbishop under section 9 of the *Synod Act 1972* following the date of the agreement under sub-section (3), the number of lay representatives for a supported parish in the Diocesan Synod is fixed at one.

(5) If a parish ceases to be a supported parish, section 34(1) of the *Synod Act 1972* thereupon applies as if any seat to which the parish is then entitled is vacant under section 34(1)(a) of that Act.

(6) The written agreement referred to in sub-section (3) must be signed by the parties and state—
 (a) the expectations of the parties for the parish and for the arrangement;
 (b) the key performance indicators for the arrangement and how it will be evaluated;
 (c) the specific arrangements and agreed expectations regarding:
  (i) the application of all applicable laws and Diocesan legislation, including the provisions of this Act;
  (ii) governance and leadership roles;
  (iii) financial arrangements, including how profits and losses are to be allocated;
  (iv) responsibility for insurance and risk management; and
  (v) reporting and the sharing of information;
 (d) what is to happen if any party fails to adhere to the agreement;
 (e) what is to happen if a person appointed to perform any functions under this legislation given to a parish officer fails to perform the function satisfactorily;
 (f) how the arrangement may be reviewed and terminated;
 (g) how disputes are to be resolved; and
 (h) a provision that the agreement is terminated automatically on the expiration of five years from the date it was last made unless it is renewed by the parties referred to in sub-section (3).

(7) A term in an agreement that alters or modifies the operation of this Act or any other Diocesan legislation as it applies to one or more of the parties to it has effect only if the term is

set out in a schedule separately approved by the Archbishop in Council.

Division 2—Diocesan review and Diocesan management

62. Diocesan review

(1) The Archbishop in Council, on the written recommendation of any two of—

(a) the Archbishop;

(b) the relevant Regional Bishop;

(c) the relevant Archdeacon;

(d) the Registrar—

may direct and authorize the Registrar to examine the records and affairs of a parish and report to the Archbishop in Council and the churchwardens.

(2) The vicar and the parish officers must give to the Registrar or anyone appointed by the Registrar for the purpose of assisting in the examination, immediately on being requested to do so, access to and, if so requested, copies of any books, registers, accounts, bank statements, minutes (together if necessary with any signatures, codes or passwords necessary to read them) that the vicar or parish officer is by virtue of any Act of the Diocese or any law of the Commonwealth of Australia or State of Victoria, required to bring into being and retain.

63. Appointment of Diocesan manager

(1) The Registrar may apply to Archbishop in Council for the appointment of a Diocesan manager to conduct the affairs of a parish.

(2) On an application under subsection (1), the Archbishop in Council may resolve to appoint a person as Diocesan

manager of the parish subject to the terms and conditions determined by the Archbishop in Council.

(3) The resolution must specify—
   (a) the date of appointment; and
   (b) the appointee's name; and
   (c) the appointee's business address.

(4) If the appointee's name or business address changes, the appointee must immediately give written notice of the change to the Registrar.

(5) Before being appointed, the Diocesan manager must enter into a written agreement with the Registrar to be bound by the provisions of this Act and by the resolution and terms and conditions determined under sub-section (2).

(6) The Archbishop in Council must not appoint a Diocesan manager unless the Registrar certifies that following an investigation or review pursuant to this Act into the affairs of the parish or the working and financial condition of the parish—
   (a) there is a serious and continuing failure of governance, administration or legal compliance; and
   (b) the appointment is in the interests of the parishioners, the Diocese or the Anglican Church.

64. Effect of appointment of Diocesan manager

(1) On the appointment of a Diocesan manager of a parish the parish officers cease to hold office.

(2) A parish officer cannot be appointed or elected while the Diocesan manager is in office except as provided by this Division.

65. Powers of Diocesan manager

(1) A Diocesan manager of a parish has control of, and may manage, the property and affairs of the parish and, to

the same extent as the churchwardens and parish council could have done but for the appointment of the Diocesan manager—

(a) may dispose of all or part of the property of the parish;

(b) may engage or discharge a person appointed under section 29; and

(c) may perform any function and exercise any power that could be performed or exercised by:

    (i) the parish;

    (ii) the parish council or vestry of the parish;

    (iii) any parish officer; or

    (iv) subject to sub-section (2), the parishioners.

(2) This Act does not alter the entitlement of the parishioners of a parish under Diocesan management to elect lay representatives and alternate lay representatives to the Synod under the *Synod Act 1972*.

(3) To avoid doubt and without limiting sub-section (1)(c), the Diocesan manager may perform any function and exercise any power the parish or a parish officer has as trustee.

(4) Where the Archbishop in Council has placed a parish under Diocesan management, the Archbishop may vary the licence of the vicar so as to suspend specified rights and functions of the vicar in relation to the governance and administration of the parish.

(5) Sub-section (4) is in addition to and not in derogation of the rights and powers of the Archbishop in Part 5 of the *Appointments Act 1971*.

66. *Revocation of appointment*

(1) A Diocesan manager of a parish holds office until the appointment is revoked.

(2) A Diocesan manager's appointment is revoked if—

(a) on application by the Registrar, the Archbishop in Council resolves to revoke the appointment of a Diocesan manager from a specified date; or

(b) the parish is discontinued under Division 3.

(3) Immediately on the revocation of a Diocesan manager's appointment, the Diocesan manager must submit to the Registrar a report showing how the Diocesan management was carried out.

(4) For the purposes of preparing the report the Diocesan manager has access to the records and documents of the parish.

(5) The Registrar may provide a copy of the report to the parish.

(6) On submitting the report under subsection (3) and accounting fully in relation to the Diocesan management of the parish to the satisfaction of the Registrar, the Diocesan manager is released from any further duty to account in relation to the Diocesan management of the parish other than on account of fraud, dishonesty, negligence or wilful failure to comply with this Act or the regulations.

(7) Before revoking the appointment of a Diocesan manager of a parish, the Archbishop in Council must—

(a) appoint another Diocesan manager; or

(b) be satisfied that the churchwardens and parish council have been elected in accordance with its parish rules for meetings and officers at a meeting convened by the Diocesan manager in accordance with those rules; or

(c) be satisfied that the Registrar has appointed churchwardens and a parish council under subsection (8).

(8) The Registrar may appoint the churchwardens, parish

council and members of the incumbency committee of a parish for which a Diocesan manager is appointed.

(9) Parish officers elected or appointed in accordance with this section—

(a) take office on revocation of the Diocesan manager's appointment; and

(b) hold office, subject to section 69, until the next annual meeting of the parish after that revocation.

67. Expenses of Diocesan management

The Archbishop in Council is authorized to pay out of church funds the fees of the Diocesan manager agreed at the time of their appointment and the expenses of and incidental to the conduct of a parish's affairs incurred by a Diocesan manager.

68. Liabilities arising from Diocesan management

(1) If a parish incurs any loss because of any fraud, dishonesty, negligence or wilful failure to comply with this Act or the regulations or the rules of the parish by a Diocesan manager, the Diocesan manager is liable for the loss.

(2) A Diocesan manager is not liable for any loss that is not a loss to which subsection (1) applies but must account for the loss in a report given under section 66(3) or 69.

69. Diocesan manager to report to Registrar

(1) On the receipt of a request from the Registrar, a Diocesan manager must, without delay, prepare and give to the Registrar a report showing how the Diocesan management is being carried out.

(2) The Registrar may give a copy of the report to the parish.

70. Additional powers of Registrar

(1) If the Registrar appoints parish officers under section 65(8), the Registrar may, at the direction of the Archbishop in Council and by written notice given to the parish, specify—

(a) a time during which this section is to apply in relation to the parish;
(b) the terms and conditions on which all or any of the parish officers hold office; and
(c) the parish rules for meetings and officers applicable to that parish.

(2) While this section applies to a parish, the Registrar may at the direction of the Archbishop in Council—
(a) from time to time remove and appoint parish officers;
(b) from time to time, vary, revoke or specify new terms and conditions in place of all or any of the terms and conditions specified under subsection (1)(b); and
(c) amend all or any of the rules specified under subsection (1)(c) in a manner permitted by section 16(2).

(3) The Registrar may, at the direction of the Archbishop in Council and by written notice given to the parish, extend the time for which this section is to apply in relation to the parish.

(4) A rule for meetings and officers specified by the Registrar under this section as a rule of a parish—
(a) is not to be altered except in the way set out in this section; and
(b) if it is inconsistent with any other rule of the parish, prevails over the other rule, and the other rule is to the extent of the inconsistency invalid; and
(c) is a rule of the parish for the purposes of this Act.

Division 3—Discontinuing a parish

71. *The purpose of this Division*

The purpose of this Division is to provide for a process by which the Archbishop in Council may for good cause designate a parish a parish under consideration and discontinue a parish under consideration in a manner that is orderly, constructive and respectful of parishioners and their faith community and that honours so far as reasonably possible those serving the mission of the Church in the parish.

72. Parishes under consideration

(1) The Archbishop in Council, at the request of a parish by resolution of a statutory parish meeting or on the written recommendation of any two of—
   (a) the Archbishop;
   (b) the relevant Regional Bishop;
   (e) the relevant Archdeacon;
   (d) the Registrar—

   may designate a parish a parish under consideration.

(2) A decision under sub-section (1) must take into account, in addition to the recommendations made, the results of any periodic review under section 55 or Diocesan review under section 62 and any recent information regarding—
   (a) the number of parishioners;
   (b) the number of baptisms;
   (c) the income of the parish and the sources of that income (and in particular whether it is from the giving or fundraising activity of parishioners or from other sources);
   (d) the solvency of a parish;
   (e) whether the buildings and grounds are properly maintained;
   (f) the parish's ability to pay its annual diocesan assessment;
   (g) the ability of the parish to fill parish offices and other lay leadership positions;

(h) the mission of the parish;
(i) whether the parish has a Mission Action Plan and its adherence to and success in pursuing that plan;
(j) any other matters prescribed in a protocol made under this division.

73. Protocol in relation to a parish under consideration

(1) The Archbishop in Council may from time to time prescribe a protocol for the steps required to be taken for the purposes of this Division in relation to a parish under consideration.

(2) Without limiting the generality of sub-section (1), the protocol may—

(a) outline a process leading to the designation of a parish as a parish under consideration;

(b) determine the criteria and indicators that a statutory parish meeting and the Archbishop in Council must have regard to in deciding whether the parish is to be discontinued;

(c) identify the information that is to be made available to the statutory parish meeting or the Archbishop in Council;

(d) determine a process for the appointment of a diocesan authority (with or without the power of delegation):

(i) to have oversight of the implementation of the protocol in relation to the parish; and

(ii) to make recommendations to the parish council, the parishioners or the Archbishop in Council as may be necessary or appropriate;

(e) determine a process by which to determine:

(i) whether the parish can and should be merged with a neighbouring parish;

(ii) how, if the parish is merged or discontinued,

the boundaries of the parish and of any neighbouring parishes should be altered so as to include the geographic area of the parish; and

(iii) how, if the parish is merged or discontinued, its property, assets and liabilities should be distributed, realized or disposed of—

and by which to consult with and establish formally the views of the parish officers and parishioners of all the neighbouring parishes regarding these matters; and

(f) determine a process for the appointment of a consultant to the parish during the implementation of the protocol whose role will be to provide advice and pastoral support to the parish in relation to all matters relating to the future of the parish, in conjunction with the vicar and the diocesan authority nominated in accordance with the protocol.

74. Duties of the parish council

(1) The parish council must within 60 days of the resolution of the Archbishop in Council under sub-section 72(1) set a period, not less than one year and not greater than three years, for the purposes of section 75.

(2) The parish council may from time to time with the approval of the Archbishop in Council abridge or extend the period fixed under the preceding sub-section.

(3) If the parish council has not within 60 days complied with sub-section (1), the Archbishop in Council must set the period and may from time to time abridge or extend the period fixed.

(4) A period as abridged or extended under sub-section (2) or (3) may be less than one year or more than three years.

(5) The parish council must carry out any steps required of it by a protocol prescribed under section 73.

75. Statutory parish meeting

(1) The parish must convene a statutory parish meeting within four months of the end of the period set under section 74.

(2) At the statutory parish meeting convened under sub-section (1) the parish must consider—

(a) a report by the appointed diocesan authority referred to in section 73(2)(d);

(b) any recommendation of the parish council; and

(c) any submissions by the vicar or any parishioner—

and vote on separate motions for the following questions:

(d) whether to petition the Archbishop in Council to discontinue the parish;

(e) whether to petition the Archbishop in Council to become a supported parish under section 60; and

(f) whether to petition the Archbishop in Council to determine that the parish is no longer a parish under consideration.

(3) A resolution to petition the Archbishop in Council to discontinue the parish must be carried by a majority of at least 75% of the total number of parishioners.

76. Decision by Archbishop in Council

(1) Within three months of receiving a petition under section 75 to discontinue a parish, the Archbishop in Council must—

(a) discontinue the parish; or

(b) determine that the parish is no longer a parish under consideration and designate the parish a supported parish under section 61.

(2) Subject to section 78, within three months of receiving a petition under section 75(2)(e) to determine that the parish

is no longer a parish under consideration and designate the parish a supported parish under section 61, if the parish has not also petitioned the Archbishop to discontinue the parish under section 75, the Archbishop in Council—

(a) must determine that the parish is no longer a parish under consideration; and

(b) may designate the parish a supported parish under section 61.

77. Other circumstances for decision by the Archbishop in Council

(1) If—

(a) the parish under consideration fails to hold the statutory parish meeting within five months of the end of the period set under section 74;

(b) the parish holds the statutory parish meeting at which the separate motions referred to in section 75(2) are not put and voted on; or

(c) at a statutory parish meeting under section 75 a motion to petition the Archbishop in Council to discontinue the parish is carried by a percentage of the total number of parishioners equal to or greater than 50 per cent and less than 75 per cent—

the Archbishop in Council must within three months:

(d) discontinue the parish;

(e) determine that the parish is no longer a parish under consideration and designate the parish a supported parish under section 61; or

(f) determine that the parish is no longer a parish under consideration.

(2) If—

(a) none of the circumstances in sub-section (1) has arisen; and

(b) none of the motions referred to in section 75(2) has been carried or the only motion to be carried is the motion referred to in section 75(2)(f)—

the parish ceases to be a parish under consideration at the expiration of seven months after the period set under section 74.

78. Matters the Archbishop in Council must consider

In making a decision under sections 76 or 77, the Archbishop in Council must consider—

- (a) any petition from the parish;
- (b) a report by the appointed diocesan authority referred to in section 73(2)(d);
- (c) any recommendation of the parish council to the statutory parish meeting; and
- (d) any written submission by the vicar, the parish council or a parishioner received by the Registrar.

79. Boundaries and assets on discontinuation of a parish

(1) At the time of making a decision to discontinue a parish under sections 76 or 77, the Archbishop in Council must revoke the declaration given under section 6 and—

- (a) merge the parish with a neighbouring parish;
- (b) redefine the boundaries of one or more neighbouring parishes so that the whole of the geographic area of the former parish is within a parish; or
- (c) both merge the parish with a neighbouring parish and alter the boundaries of one or more of the neighbouring parishes so that the whole of the geographic area of the former parish is within a parish.

(2) At the time of making a decision to discontinue a parish under sections 76 or 77 and to merge the parish or redefine

its boundaries under sub-section (1), the Archbishop in Council must—

(a) specify the date from which the parish is discontinued;

(b) decide how the property, assets and liabilities of the discontinued parish are to be distributed, realized and disposed of; and

(c) determine such other matters, and make such other provisions, as seem necessary in relation to the accounts, records and other affairs of the parish.

(3) In deciding or determining any matter under sub-section (2), the Archbishop in Council must take account of any recommendation by—

(a) the consultant;

(b) a statutory parish meeting of the parish; or

(c) the parish council—

and must make its decision or determination—

(d) having regard to the legal rights of any person under section 37(8); and

(e) in a way that:
   (i) is pastorally sensitive; and
   (ii) honours, so far as is reasonably possible, those who have given to the parish in the past and the basis on which what they have given has been received.

PART 8—RESOLUTION OF DISPUTES

80. Definition

In this Part—

parish decision means, in relation to a decision, action or function that is not spiritual—

(a) a decision or action by a diocesan authority under a

provision in this Act (including sections 81 and 82); and

(b) a failure or alleged failure by a diocesan authority:
- (i) to follow a process provided for in this Act;
- (ii) to honour a commitment to a parish on which significant reliance has been placed by the parish; or
- (iii) to adhere to the rules of natural justice in making a decision or deciding on a course of action.

81. Irregularities in parish governance

(1) If the vicar or a parish officer fails or allegedly fails to follow a requirement or process in this Act or a parish's parish rules for meetings and officers, the Archbishop in Council may take whatever steps it deems necessary and appropriate to correct or overcome the consequences of that failure or alleged failure.

(2) The steps that the Archbishop in Council may take include, but are not limited to—

(a) holding a meeting, conducting an election or making an appointment;

(b) extending the time (whether or not it has expired) within which an act may be done;

(c) declaring any decision, action, process or appointment valid despite any irregularity or omission;

(d) appointing a person to conduct an election or do any other thing;

(e) appointing sufficiently qualified persons to constitute a parish council until the churchwardens and members of a parish council have been elected or appointed under the parish's parish rules for meetings and officers;

(f) annulling any previous election, appointment, action or decision, but only to the extent necessary to enable the consequences of the original failure to be overcome or corrected.

(3) The Archbishop in Council may settle and determine all doubts and disputes that may arise with reference to—

(a) the election of any parish officer;

(b) the transaction of business by parish officers—

and may from time to time make or alter regulations, not inconsistent with this Act and with a parish's parish rules for meetings and officers, for the conducting of elections and transaction of business and may also settle and determine all doubts and disputes in relation to those matters.

82. Grievances relating to the parish electoral roll and election of Synod representatives

(1) A person aggrieved by—

(a) any enrolment or refusal of enrolment on the roll of a parish; or

(b) the removal of any name or the refusal to remove any name from the roll of a parish; or

(c) the allowance or disallowance of any vote given or tendered as a result of grievance in relation to any such enrolment, removal or refusal—

may within 14 days of the person first becoming aware of the facts or circumstances giving rise to the grievance appeal in writing to the Archbishop in Council.

(2) The Archbishop in Council may appoint a person to gather such evidence and material as is necessary for it to consider and decide the appeal.

(3) The decision of the Archbishop in Council on an appeal is final.

(4) The Archbishop in Council may extend the time within which an appeal may be given under this section.

(5) Every appeal in respect of an election held under the *Synod Act 1972* for the election of lay representatives or alternative lay representatives must be determined by the Election Committee established under that Act.

83. Parish Decision Mediation Panel

(1) There is established a Parish Disputes Mediation Panel.

(2) The panel comprises between 5 and 8 persons appointed by the Archbishop in Council for a period of 4 years who—

    (a) are members of a Christian denomination;

    (b) have qualifications and experience in mediation and alternative dispute resolution; and

    (c) have not at the time of their appointment been in the preceding 3 years within the Diocese:

        (i) a member of the Council of the Diocese;

        (ii) a member of a Regional Council;

        (iii) an Archbishop, Regional Bishop, Archdeacon or area dean; or

        (iv) Chancellor, Deputy Chancellor, or Advocate; or

        (v) the Registrar or a member of the Diocesan staff.

84. Mediation

(1) A parish officer may make a complaint in relation to a parish decision (other than a parish decision under sections 76 or 77).

(2) A complaint under sub-section (1) must in the first instance be given in writing to the Registrar.

(3) On receiving a complaint under sub-section (1) the

Registrar must refer it to the member of the Parish Dispute Mediation Panel next in line by rotation.

(4) The mediator must attempt to resolve the complaint within 60 days.

85. Provisions in support of this Part

(1) The Diocese must provide the funds and facilities necessary for the work of the Parish Disputes Mediation Panel.

(2) So far as is possible the Parish Disputes Mediation Panel will be supported by the Registry of the Diocese. The Registrar must ensure that this support is entirely separate from any function of the Registry concerned with the participation of the Diocese and its authorities and agents in any mediation.

PART 9—GENERAL

86. Extent of liability of parish officers and others

(1) In this section, a reference to this Act is a reference to this Act or the regulations made under it or the applicable parish rules.

(2) To the extent permitted by law, a diocesan authority, vicar, parish officer or treasurer shall not be personally liable for any loss occasioned by the exercise of any discretion or power conferred on that person under this Act or by that person's failure to comply with any duty responsibility or obligation under this Act other than a loss attributable to that person's—

(a) fraud or dishonesty; or

(b) wilful failure to comply with this Act or other wilful misconduct.

87. Regulations

(1) The Archbishop in Council may make regulations for or

with respect to any matter or thing required or permitted by this Act to be prescribed or necessary to be prescribed to give effect to this Act.

(2) Without limiting subsection (1), the Archbishop in Council may make regulations for or with respect to—

(a) sections 33(6) and 72(1);

(b) any matter that may be prescribed under section 21(1), 30, 31(1), 32(1), 34(2), 34(7), 36(3), 37(8), 45(1), 47(1), 52(2), 55(3) and 73(2);

(c) the matters to be addressed by a statutory parish meeting held for the purposes of Parts 6 or 7; and

(d) any forms required by Division 1 of Part 4.

(3) Regulations made under this Act may—

(a) be of general or limited application;

(b) differ according to differences in time, place or circumstance;

(c) confer a discretionary authority or impose a duty on a specified person or body or a specified class of person or body.

(4) The power to make regulations includes the power to amend or revoke them.

88. Parish Governance (Transitions, Consequential Amendments and Repeals) Act 2013 to prevail

A provision of the *Parish Governance (Transitions, Consequential Amendments and Repeals) Act 2013* prevails over an inconsistent provision in this Act.

Schedule 1
Parish rules for meetings and officers

Note: Under section 16(2) of the Parish Governance Act 2013, a statutory parish meeting may adopt modified parish rules for meetings and officers only to the extent that the text is permitted text in this Schedule and the permitted text is used in conformity with the instructions relating to that text in this Schedule.

Parish rules for Meetings and Officers applying to the Parish by virtue of Division 2 of Part 4 of the *Parish Governance Act 2013*

1. Definition

1.1 In these rules—

the Act means the Parish Governance Act 2013;

member of the immediate family of an individual means a person who is:

(a) a parent, child or sibling of the individual;

(b) a spouse or domestic partner of the individual; or

(c) a relative of the individual and a member of the individual's household.

1.2 Words and expressions in these rules have the same meaning as in the Act.

2. Notices of statutory parish meetings

2.1 The churchwardens must give parishioners at least 14 days' notice of any statutory parish meeting.

2.2 On receiving a notice of special meeting under rule 4.2, the churchwardens must fix a date and time for the meeting that is

2.3 not less than 5 weeks or more than 8 weeks from the date of that notice, and immediately give notice of the meeting.

2.3 At a time when it becomes necessary to convene a special election meeting under rule 5, the churchwardens must fix a date and time for the meeting that is not less than 3 weeks or more than 6 weeks from that time and immediately give notice of the meeting.

2.4 Each notice of a statutory parish meeting must give the date, time and place of the meeting, and the business to be transacted at the meeting.

2.5 Notice of a statutory parish meeting must be displayed prominently on or near the main entrance to each worship centre and where necessary it must be given or distributed in other ways that are likely to inform parishioners of the meeting.

Addition to rule 2		
No.	Permitted text	Instructions
A.1	2.6 In addition to the requirements of rule 2.5— * notice of any statutory parish meeting # * notice of nominations for election # * proposed modified parish rules for meetings and officers # and * papers to be distributed at the meeting # must be: * sent by post to all parishioners ☾ * posted on the parish website ☾ * posted on the parish website accessible only to parishioners ☾ * sent as an email attachment to all parishioners ☾	#—select one or more ☾—select one or more

3. Annual meeting

3.1   The annual meeting must be held in October or November of each year on a date and at a time fixed by the parish council.

3.2   A notice of an annual meeting must state the time and date by which nominations for election are to be received by the vicar. The time and date fixed for the receipt of nominations must be—

   (a) at least 96 hours before the time fixed for the commencement of the annual meeting; and

   (b) before the time of the first service held on the Sunday immediately preceding the meeting.

Alternative to rule 3.2 (second sentence)		
No.	Permitted text	Instructions
B.1	In place of "96 hours" insert "[X] days"	[X] must be a whole number between 5 and 10

3.3   All nominations for election must be displayed at or near the main entrance to the worship centre for at least 48 hours before the time fixed for the commencement of the annual meeting.

Alternative to rule 3.3		
No.	Permitted text	Instructions
C.1	In place of "48 hours" insert "[X] hours or [Y] days"	[X] or [Y] must be a whole number, and the period must be greater than 48 hours and less than the period in rule 3.2

3.4 The business of the annual meeting is to include after prayers—
(a) The minutes of the previous annual meeting and of any subsequent statutory parish meeting;
(b) The reception of the parish electoral roll;
(c) The annual report by the vicar that includes the entries in the registers of the Parish for the financial year, including numbers of baptisms, persons received into communicant membership, confirmations, marriages, funerals, Sunday services, acts of communion and such other statistics from the registers as Archbishop in Council determines;
(d) An annual report on the proceedings of the parish council and together with a report by the parish council on the pastoral care, evangelism, social and ecumenical programmes of the parish and on future plans for the parish;
(e) A report by the churchwardens on the fabric, goods and ornaments of the worship centre and the vicarage and other buildings of the parish;
(f) The audited or independently examined accounts and financial statements of the parish and any accompanying papers required by the Act;
(g) The budget approved by the parish council for the year in which the meeting is held;
(h) Reports by other parish groups;
(i) The election of churchwardens and members of the parish council;
(j) The election of an auditor or independent examiner;
(k) The election of lay representatives to the parish incumbency committee and of the incumbency committee reserve list;
(l) Any other matters of parochial or general church interest.

4. Special meetings
4.1 A special meeting is convened—

(a) if the majority of the whole number of members of the parish council so decides;

(b) at the request of at least two churchwardens; or

(c) on the written request of at least 20 parishioners.

Alternative to rule 4.1(c)		
No.	Permitted text	Instructions
D.1	(c) on the written request of at least [X] parishioners	[X] can be a percentage (e.g. 25% of...) or any whole number, but in either case the number required must be not less than 10 or greater than one-third of the number of parishioners

4.2 A decision or request to convene a special meeting must be given in writing to the churchwardens, the vicar and the parish secretary and state the matters to be put to the meeting.

4.3 The business of a special meeting is to include only the matters referred to in the decision or request referred to in rule 4.2.

5. Special election meetings

5.1 A special election meeting is convened in the event that the number of lay members of the parish council falls to less than half the total number of elected and appointed members under rule 10.1.

Alternative to rule 5.1		
No.	Permitted text	Instructions
E.1	5.1 A special election is convened in the event that the number of lay members of the parish council falls to a number less than [X]	[X] must be a whole number equal to or greater than the number of elected and appointed members under rule 10.1

5.2 The business of a special election meeting is to fill any casual vacancies in the positions of elected churchwardens or members of the parish council.

5.3 The provisions of rules 3.2 and 3.3 apply to the nomination of parishioners to fill casual vacancies at a special election meeting.

6. Entitlement to be present and vote at statutory parish meetings

6.1 A parishioner is entitled to be present and vote at a statutory parish meeting.

6.2 A clerk who regularly and habitually attends public worship in the parish and a member of staff of the parish who is not a parishioner is entitled to be present at a statutory parish meeting and to speak by leave of the meeting, but not to vote.

6.3 A person other than a parishioner and a person referred to in rule 6.2 may not be present or speak at a statutory parish meeting except in each case by leave of the meeting.

7. Procedure at statutory parish meetings

7.1 The vicar presides at a statutory parish meeting and does not have a vote.

7.2 A question will be determined by the majority of the votes of the parishioners present and voting on the question, and in the event of an equality of votes a question is resolved in the negative.

7.3 A quorum at a statutory parish meeting of a parish is 10 parishioners or one-fifth the number of parishioners on the parish electoral roll, whichever is greater.

Alternative to rule 7.3		
No.	Permitted text	Instructions
F.1	7.3 A quorum at a statutory parish meeting of a parish is [X] parishioners or one-fifth the number of parishioners on the parish electoral roll, whichever is greater	[X] must be greater than 10

F.2	7.3 A quorum at a statutory parish meeting of a parish is 10 parishioners or [insert proportion] the number of parishioners on the parish electoral roll, whichever is greater	Proportion must be greater than one-fifth
F.3	7.3 A quorum at a statutory parish meeting of a parish is [X] parishioners or [insert proportion] the number of parishioners on the parish electoral roll, whichever is greater	[X] must be greater than 10 and the proportion must be greater than one-fifth

7.4 If a quorum is not present within half an hour after the time fixed for the holding of a statutory parish meeting, or if during a meeting there is a call of the meeting and there is no quorum, the meeting lapses and a statutory parish meeting may be convened to consider such of the business as was not dealt with at the earlier meeting.

7.5 If a statutory parish meeting lapses before voting has been completed for an election to be held at the meeting, the vicar must convene a further statutory parish meeting to hold the election.

8. Nominations for election

8.1 At the time when an annual meeting is called there must be a call for nominations for—
   (a) churchwardens;
   (b) elected members of the parish council; and
   (c) members of the incumbency committee and the incumbency committee reserve list.

8.2 Nominations must be in writing and signed by—
   (a) the person nominated;
   (b) the proposer; and
   (c) the seconder,
each of whom must be a parishioner and not a disqualified person.

8.3 If the person nominated is unable to sign the nomination, there may be a statement signed by the proposer and seconder to the effect that the person nominated has consented to the nomination.

8.4 Where there is no nomination for a position (including where the number of vacancies exceeds the number of nominations) there is a casual vacancy in that position.

9. Conduct of elections

9.1 If at the time of any election the number of candidates is not greater than the number of vacancies the candidates nominated shall be declared elected.

9.2 If an election is required it will be by secret ballot conducted by a returning officer appointed by the vicar.

9.3 If in an election there is an equality of votes requiring casting vote, the returning officer may at his or her discretion exercise a casting vote or determine the result by lot.

10. Parish council

10.1 The parish council consists of—

(a) the vicar;

(b) three churchwardens; and

(c) 9 other persons, one-third nominated by the vicar and two-thirds elected by the parishioners.

Alternative to rule 10.1 (b) and (c)		
No.	Permitted text	Instructions
G.1	(b) 3 churchwardens; and (c) 3 other persons, one-third nominated by the vicar and two-thirds elected by the parishioners	
G.2	(b) 3 churchwardens and (c) 6 other persons, one-third nominated by the vicar and two-thirds elected by the parishioners	

G.3	(b) three churchwardens and (c) 12 other persons, one-third nominated by the vicar and two-thirds elected by the parishioners	
G.4	(b) 3 churchwardens (c) the treasurer, elected by the annual meeting and (d) 2 other persons, one nominated by the vicar and one elected by the parishioners	Must not be used with option P.1 and option P.2 must be used
G.5	(b) 3 churchwardens (c) the treasurer, elected by the annual meeting, and (d) 5 other persons, 2 nominated by the vicar and 3 elected by the parishioners	Must not be used with option P.1 and option P.2 must be used
G.6	(b) 3 churchwardens (c) the treasurer, elected by the annual meeting, and (d) 8 other persons, 3 nominated by the vicar and 5 elected by the parishioners	Must not be used with option P.1 and option P.2 must be used
G.7	(b) 3 churchwardens (c) the treasurer, elected by the annual meeting, and (d) 11 other persons, 4 nominated by the vicar and 7 elected by the parishioners.	Must not be used with option P.1 and option P.2 must be used
G.8	(b) 3 churchwardens (c) the parish secretary, elected by the annual meeting, and (d) 2 other persons, 1 nominated by the vicar and 1 elected by the parishioners	Must not be used with option Q.1 and option Q.2 must be used

G.9	(b) 3 churchwardens (c) the parish secretary, elected by the annual meeting, and (d) 5 other persons, 2 nominated by the vicar and 3 elected by the parishioners	Must not be used with option Q.1 and option Q.2 must be used
G.10	(b) 3 churchwardens (c) the parish secretary, elected by the annual meeting, and (d) 8 other persons, 3 nominated by the vicar and 5 elected by the parishioners	Must not be used with option Q.1 and option Q.2 must be used
G.11	(b) 3 churchwardens; (c) the parish secretary, elected by the annual meeting, and (d) 11 other persons, 4 nominated by the vicar and 7 elected by the parishioners.	Must not be used with option Q1 and option Q.2 must be used
G.12	(b) 3 churchwardens (c) the treasurer, elected by the annual meeting; (d) the parish secretary, elected by the annual meeting; and (e) 1 other person nominated by the vicar	Must not be used with options P.1 or Q.1 and options P.2 and Q.2 must be used
G.13	(b) three churchwardens (c) the treasurer, elected by the annual meeting (d) the parish secretary, elected by the annual meeting, and (e) 4 other persons, 2 nominated by the vicar and 2 elected by the parishioners	Must not be used with options P.1 or Q.1 and options P.2 and Q.2 must be used

G.14	(b) 3 churchwardens (c) the treasurer, elected by the annual meeting; (d) the parish secretary, elected by the annual meeting, and (e) 7 other persons, 3 nominated by the vicar and 4 elected by the parishioners	Must not be used with options P.1 or Q.1 and options P.2 and Q.2 must be used
G.15	(b) three churchwardens (c) the treasurer, elected by the annual meeting; (d) the parish secretary, elected by the annual meeting, and (e) 10 other persons, 4 nominated by the vicar and 6 elected by the parishioners	Must not be used with options P.1 or Q.1 and options P.2 and Q.2 must be used

10.2   The parish council may co-opt a parishioner (other than a person who is not eligible for election or appointment under rule 13) to assist the council for such a period (but not extending beyond the conclusion of the next parish annual meeting) as the council determines and such person shall have a right to attend and speak at but not vote at meetings of the Council.

Alternative to rule 10.2		
No.	Permitted text	Instructions
H.1	10.2 *Omitted*	This option must be used with options N.2 or N.3

10.3   A clerk in holy orders licensed or authorized for service in the parish or a stipendiary lay person appointed to the parish who is not otherwise a member of the council may attend and speak but not vote at meetings of the parish council.

Alternative to rule 10.3			
No.	**Permitted text**	**Instructions**	
I.1	10.3 A clerk in holy orders licensed or authorized for service in the parish, a stipendiary lay person appointed to the parish who is not otherwise a member of the council, and any of the following office holders (unless they are not eligible for election or appointment under rule 13) * [title of office or position] * [title of office or position] may attend and speak but not vote at meetings of the parish council	Insert the title of each position e.g. director of music, youth outreach coordinator	

10.4   The parish council may invite any person (whether or not a parishioner, but other than a person who is not eligible for election or appointment under rule 13.2) to attend and speak but not vote at a meeting of the council.

Permitted rule 10.5		
No.	**Permitted text**	**Instructions**
J.1	10.5 Any parishioner may attend (but not speak except by invitation of the council) a meeting of the council other than a portion of the meeting that the council determines is closed to people who are not members of the council or entitled to be present under [rules 10.2 and 10.3]	[text] to read rule 10.3 if option H.1 is used

183

11. Quorum

11.1   A majority of the parish council constitutes the quorum.

Alternative to rule 11.1		
No.	Permitted text	Instructions
K.1	11.1 [X] members of the parish council constitutes a quorum	[X] must be a whole number greater than half the number of members of the parish council

12. Term of office

12.1   A churchwarden or member of the parish council—

    (a) appointed by the vicar; or

    (b) appointed by the parish council or elected by a special election meeting—

holds office until the conclusion of the annual meeting next following that election or appointment.

12.2   A churchwarden elected at an annual meeting holds office until the conclusion of the annual meeting next following that election.

Alternative to rule 12.2		
No.	Permitted text	Instructions
L.1	12.2 A churchwarden elected at an annual meeting holds office until the conclusion of the second annual meeting following the election, but if two churchwardens are elected at the same annual meeting, one of them (determined by them jointly or, in the absence of agreement, by lot) must retire at the conclusion of the next annual meeting	

12.3　A member of the parish council at an annual meeting holds office until the conclusion of the annual meeting next following that election.

\multicolumn{3}{l}{Alternative to rule 12.3}		
No.	Permitted text	Instructions
M.1	12.3 A member of the parish council (other than a churchwarden) elected at an annual meeting holds office until the conclusion of the second annual meeting following that election 12.4 If the number of members of the parish council (other than the churchwardens) elected at an annual meeting is greater than half the total number of elected members of the parish council (other than the churchwardens), so many of them (other than a treasurer or parish secretary so elected) as equals the difference between half the total number of elected members of the parish council (other than the churchwardens) and the number so elected (determined by them jointly or, in the absence of agreement, by lot) must retire at the conclusion of the next annual meeting	

13. Eligibility for election

13.1　A person is not eligible for election or appointment as a churchwarden or member of the parish council if the person is not a communicant member.

13.2　Subject to rule 13.3, a person who has been for a continuous period of six years in any capacity a lay member of the parish council in the parish (including a person co-opted under rule 10.2) is not eligible for election or appointment as a churchwarden or member of the parish council, or to become a member of the parish council by election or appointment as a treasurer or parish secretary, at any time in the 12 months immediately following that six year period.

Alternative to rule 13.2		
No.	Permitted text	Instructions
N.1	13.2 Subject to rule 13.3, a person who has been for a continuous period of [X] years in any capacity a lay member of the parish council in the parish (including a person co-opted under rule 10.2) is not eligible for election or appointment as a churchwarden or member of the parish council, or to become a member of the parish council by election or appointment as a treasurer or parish secretary, at any time in the [Y] months immediately following that [X] year period	(1) [X] cannot be greater than 6 and [Y] cannot be less than 12 and must be divisible by 12. (2) If alternative 12.2.1 or 12.2.2 has been used, [X] must be an even number
N.2	13.2 Subject to rule 13.3, a person who has been for a continuous period of six years in any capacity a lay member of the parish council in the parish is not eligible for election or appointment as a churchwarden or member of the parish council, or to become a member of the parish council by election or appointment as a treasurer or parish secretary, at any time in the 12 months immediately following that six year period	This option or N.3 must be used if cl 10.2 is omitted, but not otherwise

N.3	13.2 Subject to rule 13.3, a person who has been for a continuous period of [X] years in any capacity a lay member of the parish council in the parish is not eligible for election or appointment as a churchwarden or member of the parish council, or to become a member of the parish council by election or appointment as a treasurer or parish secretary, at any time in the [Y] months immediately following that [X] year period	This option or N.2 must be used if cl 10.2 is omitted, but not otherwise (1) [X] cannot be greater than 6 and [Y] cannot be less than 12 and must be divisible by 12 (2) If alternative 12.2.1 or 12.2.2 has been used, [X] must be an even number

13.3　A person is not ineligible under rule 13.2 for election or appointment at or following an annual meeting if they have not been in any capacity a lay member of the parish council since the conclusion of the previous annual meeting.

13.4　A disqualified person within the meaning of the Act is not eligible for election or appointment as a parish officer.

14. Termination of office

14.1　The office of a churchwarden or member of the parish council becomes vacant if he or she —

   (a) is absent for three consecutive meetings of the council except on leave of absence granted by the council; or

   (b) fails to sign a declaration as required by section 20 of the Act; or

   (c) resigns in writing to the vicar; or

(d) ceases to be a parishioner; or

(e) becomes a disqualified person.

14.2   The office of a churchwarden becomes vacant if he or she at any time—

(a) holds a remunerated office or position in the parish without the consent referred to in section 27(4) of the Act;

(b) is or becomes a member of the immediate family of the incumbent; or

(c) is or becomes the treasurer of the parish otherwise than under rule 18.2(b).

14.3   Acceptance by a council of an apology for absence from a meeting of the parish council is to be taken to be a grant of leave of absence from that meeting.

Alternative to rule 14.3		
No.	Permitted text	Instructions
O.1	14.3 Omitted	

15. Casual vacancies

15.1   Where there is a vacancy in an office of churchwarden or member of the parish council appointed by the vicar, the vicar may nominate a person eligible to fill the vacancy.

15.2   Subject to rule 15.5, where there is a vacancy in an elected office of churchwarden or member of the parish council, the remaining members of the parish council may fill the vacancy by a person eligible to fill the vacancy.

15.3   A person nominated or elected pursuant to this section holds office for the remainder of the term of office of the person whose place is being filled.

15.4   The validity of anything done by a parish council is not affected by a vacancy in the membership of the council for as long as the number of lay members of the parish council (inclusive of the churchwardens) is greater than half the number provided for in rule 10.1.

15.5 If the number of lay members of the parish council (inclusive of the churchwardens) is equal to or less than half the number of lay members (inclusive of the churchwardens) provided for in rule 10.1, the parish council cannot make any decisions or undertake any action other than what is necessary to convene a special election meeting.

15.6 Despite any other provision in these rules, the churchwardens or the remaining churchwarden or churchwardens may continue to discharge all the powers and functions vested in them by the Act and these rules notwithstanding the number of vacancies in the parish council.

16. Chairing meetings of the parish council

16.1. The chair of a meeting of the parish council is—

    (a) the vicar or a member of the parish council nominated by the vicar; or

    (b) if vicar or person so nominated is not present, a member of the parish council chosen by the parish council.

17. Churchwardens

17.1 The parish has three churchwardens, two elected by the parishioners and one appointed by the vicar.

18. Parish treasurer

18.1 The parish treasurer is appointed by the churchwardens.

Alternative to rule 18.1		
No.	Permitted text	Instructions
P.1	18.1 The parish treasurer is appointed by the parish council	This may be used if options G.4, G.5, G.6, G.7, G.12, G.13, G.14, and G.15 are *not* used

P.2	18.1 Omitted	This must be used if option G.4, G.5, G.6, G.7, G.12, G.13, G.14, or G.15 is used

18.2 The treasurer—

    (a) must be a parishioner; and

    (b) except with the prior agreement of, and for such period and on such other terms set by, the Archbishop in Council, must not be a churchwarden.

18.3 If the person appointed as treasurer is not a member of the council, he or she becomes, upon being so appointed, a member of the council for all purposes for the remainder of the current term of the council.

18.4 The treasurer is responsible to the churchwardens for–

    (a) ensuring the proper banking of all moneys of the parish and the proper payment of all amounts payable by the parish;

    (b) maintaining proper financial records of the parish;

    (c) reporting to each meeting of the parish council on the financial affairs of the parish, including projected outcomes in accordance with the annual budget of the council;

    (d) preparing forward estimates of income and expenditure in accordance with strategies and plans adopted by the council;

    (e) ensuring that the accounts of the parish are audited or assessed as required by the Act; and

    (f) preparing the annual financial report to the annual meeting.

18.5 The name and postal address of the treasurer must be given to the Registrar.

19. Parish secretary

19.1 The parish council may appoint a lay member of the parish council as parish secretary.

Alternative to rule 19.1		
No.	Permitted text	Instructions
Q.1	19.1 The churchwardens may appoint a lay member of the parish council as parish secretary	This may be used if options G.8, G.9, G.10, G.11, G.12, G.13, G.14, and G.15 are *not* used
Q.2	19.1 *Omitted*	This must be used if options G.8, G.9, G.10, G.11, G.12, G.13, G.14, and G.15 are used

19.2　The duties of the parish secretary are determined by the parish council.

Alternative to rule 19.2		
No.	Permitted text	Instructions
R.1	19.2 The parish secretary is responsible for— [*insert responsibilities e.g.* * *ensuring that minutes of statutory parish meetings are made, displayed and permanently kept;* * *sending and receiving correspondence on behalf of the parish;* * *maintaining up to date compilations of the legal requirements applying to the parish;* * *assisting the wardens and parish council to comply with their legal obligations and responsibilities*]	This may be used only if option G.8, G.9, G.10, G.11, G.12, G.13, G.14, or G.15 is used

19.3　The name and postal address of the parish secretary must be given to the Registrar.

20. Nomination by the vicar

20.1　The vicar must announce to the parishioners within 30 days of becoming entitled to appoint a person as churchwarden and or member of the parish council the name of each person appointed.

21. Acting appointments

21.1 During a period when a churchwarden or treasurer is absent or is, for any reason, unable to perform the duties of the office—

(a) the parish council may appoint one of its members to act in the place of a churchwarden elected by the parish during some or all of that period;

(b) the vicar may appoint a communicant member who is a parishioner (whether or not a member of the parish council) to act in the place of a churchwarden appointed by the vicar during some or all of that period; and

(c) the churchwardens may appoint a communicant member who is a parishioner (whether or not a member of the parish council) to act in the place of the treasurer during some or all of that period.

22. Meetings of the parish council

22.1 The parish council must hold such meetings as are necessary for the performance of its functions.

Alternative to rule 22.1		
No.	Permitted text	Instructions
S.1	22.1 The parish council must hold such meetings as are necessary for the performance of its functions and must meet at least [X] times each year.	[X] must be a whole number
S.2	22.1 The parish council must hold such meetings as are necessary for the performance of its functions and must meet at least every [insert number of months].	Insert one of the following— * month * two months * three months

22.2　A meeting of the parish council may be convened, subject to any directions of the council, at any time by the vicar or the person (if any) nominated by the vicar as its chair.

22.3　A meeting of the parish council shall be convened upon request by four of its members.

22.4　Questions arising at a meeting of the parish council shall be determined by a majority of the votes of the members present and voting and, if the votes are equal, the question shall be decided in the negative.

22.5　The person chairing a meeting of a council, has a deliberative vote but does not, in the event of an equality of votes, have a casting vote.

22.6　True and accurate records of each meeting of the parish council shall be kept and signed by the chair.

23. Conflict of interest

23.1　A member of the parish council who has a pecuniary interest in a matter before the council must—

(a) declare that interest at the first occasion on which it becomes apparent that the matter is to be discussed at, referred to or considered by the meeting;

(b) not vote on any question in relation to that matter; and

(c) if so requested by:

(i)　the chair of the meeting; or

(ii)　the meeting following a secret ballot requested by any member of the parish council (without the requirement of a seconder)—

be absent from and out of sight and hearing of the meeting during any discussion or consideration by the meeting, and during any vote in relation to the matter.

23.2　In addition to any other basis on which a member of a parish council may be considered to have a pecuniary interest in a matter, the member has a pecuniary interest if the matter concerns the financial interests of the council member, of a member of the immediate family of the council member, or of any business or organization (whether profit-making or not) of which the council member or a member of the immediate family of the council member is an office holder.

23.3 If the provisions of this rule mean that the parish council is during consideration of that matter without a quorum, the members present constitute a quorum in relation to that matter.

24. Minutes of meetings

24.1 The minutes of statutory parish meetings and of the parish council must be publicly displayed.

Schedule 2
Additional Parish rules for Meetings and Officers for a section 18 parish

25. *Local annual meeting*

25.1   If a local worship centre has decided to hold local annual meetings under section 18(2) of the Act, that local annual meeting must be held in October or November of each year on a date and at a time fixed by the parish council.

25.2   The rules relating to a statutory parish meeting apply to a local annual meeting, a local special meeting and a local special electoral meeting.

Alternative to rule 25.2		
No.	Permitted text	Instructions
U.1	25.2 The rules relating to a statutory parish meeting apply to a local annual meeting a local special meeting and a local special electoral meeting, but for the following worship centres the quorum for a local annual meeting is— * [name of worship centre]: [X] * [name of worship centre]: [Y]	(1) Only insert worship centres that have a separate annual meeting and have fewer than 30 parishioners on the local electoral roll (2) [X] and [Y] must be a whole number equal to or greater than 4 or one-third the number of parishioners on the local electoral roll (whichever is greater)

25.3   A copy of the local electoral roll displayed under section 12(1) of the Act must be presented to the local annual meeting.

25.4   The business of the local annual meeting is to include after prayers—

   (a) The minutes of the previous local annual meeting and of any subsequent local meeting;
   (b) The reception of the local electoral roll;
   (c) A report by the vicar in relation to the parish and the worship centre;
   (d) A report by the churchwardens on the buildings, fabric, fittings and grounds of the worship centre;
   (e) A report by the churchwardens on the contribution of the worship centre to the parish budget;
   (f) If the worship centre has a vestry, a report on its proceedings;
   (g) Reports by other groups associated with the worship centre;
   (h) If the worship centre has a vestry, the election of members of the vestry;
   (i) The election of a member of the incumbency committee and a member of the incumbency committee reserve list;
   (j) Any other matters of parochial or general church interest.

26. Entitlement to be present and vote at local meetings

26.1   In the case of a local annual meeting, local special meeting or local special electoral meeting, this rule operates instead of rule 6.

26.2   A parishioner on the local electoral roll of a local worship centre is entitled to be present and vote at a local annual meeting of that worship centre.

26.3   A churchwarden or treasurer of the parish and a member of staff of the parish who is not on the local electoral roll, and a clerk who regularly and habitually attends public worship at the local worship centre, is entitled to be present at a local meeting and to speak by leave of the meeting, but not to vote.

26.4   A person other than a person referred to in rules 26.2 and 26.3 may not be present or speak at a statutory parish meeting except in each case by leave of the meeting.

27. Local Vestry

27.1   If a local worship centre has decided that there is to be a vestry for that worship centre under section 18(2) of the Act, elections for the vestry are to be conducted at the local annual meeting.

27.2   A vestry of a worship centre is, under the vicar, responsible to the parish council for managing the affairs of the worship centre.

27.3   A vestry consists of—
   (a) the vicar;
   (b) the churchwardens of the parish;
   (c) the treasurer of the parish;
   (d) six other members who are parishioners on the local electoral roll, one-third nominated by the vicar and two-thirds elected by the parishioners on the local electoral roll.

27.4   A person may be at the same time a member of a vestry under rule 27.3(d) and a member of the parish council under rule 10.1(c).

27.5   A member of the vestry holds office until the conclusion of the annual meeting next following his or her election or appointment.

27.6   A person who has been a member of a vestry for a continuous period of six years in any capacity is not eligible for election or appointment as a member of a vestry at any time in the 12 months immediately following that six-year period, but is not ineligible for election or appointment at or following a local annual meeting if they have not been a member of the vestry since the conclusion of the previous local annual meeting.

27.7   A clerk in holy orders licensed or authorized for service in the parish or a stipendiary lay person appointed to the parish who is not otherwise a member of the vestry may attend and speak but not vote at meetings of a vestry.

27.8 A vestry may invite any person (whether or not on the local electoral roll of that worship centre, unless that person is not eligible under rule 27.6) to attend and speak but not to vote at a meeting of the vestry.

Alternative to rule 27.8		
No.	Permitted text	Instructions
V.1	27.8 Any parishioner on the roll of a worship centre may attend (but not speak except by invitation of the council) a meeting of the vestry of that worship centre other than a portion of the meeting that the vestry determines is closed to people who are not members of the vestry or entitled to be present under rules 27.7	

27.9 True and accurate minutes of each meeting of the vestry shall be kept and signed by the chair.

27.10 The chair of the vestry is the vicar or a person nominated by the vicar.

27.11 The vestry may appoint one of the members elected or nominated under paragraph 27.3(d) to be the vestry secretary, with such duties as the vestry determines.

27.12 A majority of the parish council (of whom at least three must be members nominated or elected under rule 27.3(d)) constitutes the quorum.

28. Application of parish rules for meetings and officers to local worship centre

28.1 Except as otherwise provided in these rules, the provisions of these rules apply, with any necessary modifications, to the meetings, elections, appointments and vestry of the local worship centre.

29. Minutes of meetings

29.1 The minutes of local statutory parish meetings and vestries must be publicly displayed.

Alternative to rule 29		
No.	Permitted text	Instructions
W.1	29.1 For the [insert name] worship centre, the minutes of local statutory parish meetings must be displayed— (a) publicly (a) on the parish's website (a) publicly and on the parish's website and the minutes of the vestry must be displayed: (b) publicly (b) on the parish's website (b) publicly and on the parish's website	(1) Insert name of worship centre (2) Only one paragraph (a) to be used (3) Only one paragraph (b) to be used
W.2	29.2 For the [insert name of some other] worship centre, the minutes of local statutory parish meetings must be displayed— (a) publicly (a) on the parish's website (a) publicly and on the parish's website and the minutes of the vestry must be displayed: (b) publicly (b) on the parish's website (b) publicly and on the parish's website	(1) Insert name of another worship centre (2) Only one paragraph (a) to be used (3) Only one paragraph (b) to be used

W.3	29.2 For the [*insert name of some other*] worship centre, the minutes of local statutory parish meetings and vestry meetings are not to be publicly displayed	This text may be used as a rule 29.2 in relation to a third worship centre, or may be used instead of the preceding rule 29.2 in the case of a second worship centre
W.4	29. *Omitted*	Where no minutes for any worship centre are to be displayed, the rule may be omitted

Schedule 3
Notes to accompany accounts

The notes to the accounts must provide the following information to the extent that it is not disclosed in the accounts—

(a) a description of each of the accounting policies that have been adopted by the churchwardens, and which are material in the context of the accounts of the parish, together with a description of those estimation techniques adopted which are material to the presentation of the accounts;

(b) a description of any material change to these policies and techniques, the reason for such change and its effect (if material) on the accounts;

(c) a description of the nature and purpose of all material funds of the parish;

(d) such particulars of the related party transactions of the parish, or of any institution or body corporate connected with the parish;

(e) a description of any incoming receipts which represent capital, according to whether or not that capital is permanent endowment;

(f) an itemized analysis of any material movement between any of the restricted funds of the parish, or between a restricted and an unrestricted funds of the parish, together with an explanation of the nature and purpose of each of those funds;

(g) the name of any institution or body corporate connected with the parish, together with a description of the nature of the parish's relationship with that institution or body corporate and of its activities;

(h) particulars of any contingent liability in the name of the parish or the churchwardens on its behalf, where any potential liability is outstanding at the date of the statement of assets and liabilities;

(i) particulars of any loan outstanding at the date of the statement of assets and liabilities:
   (i) which was made to the parish, and which is secured by an express charge on any of the assets of the parish; or
   (ii) which was made by the parish to any institution or body corporate connected with the parish;

(j) particulars of any fund of the parish, which is materially in deficit at the date of the statement of assets and liabilities;

(k) particulars of any ex gratia payment made by the parish;

(l) a statement as to whether or not the accounts have been prepared in accordance with any applicable accounting standards and statements of recommended practice and particulars of any material departure from those standards and statements of practice and the reasons for such departure.

NOTES

Amended by Parish Governance Amendment Act 2015

Amended by Melbourne Anglican Diocesan Corporation Act 2015 (not yet in force)

Diocesan Legislation Interpretation Act 2016 (deleting two definitions)

Diocesan Legislation (Revision and Repeals) Act 2016 (Schedule 1, clause 10)

Parish Governance Regulations 2014

PART 1—PRELIMINARY

1.1 Title

These regulations may be cited as the Parish Governance Regulations 2014.

1.2 Authorizing provisions

These regulations are made under section 87 of the *Parish Governance Act 2013*.

1.3 Commencement

These regulations come into effect on the day on which the *Parish Governance Act 2013* commences.

1.4 Interpretation

(1) Words and expressions in these regulations have the same meaning as in the *Parish Governance Act 2013*, and references to "**the Act**" are references to that Act.

(2) In these regulations, unless the context otherwise requires—

"**ADF**" means the Anglican Development Fund in the Diocese of Melbourne.

PART 2—FORMS RELATING TO PARISH ROLLS AND MOVEMENT BETWEEN PARISHES

2.1 Prescribed forms in relation to parish rolls

Schedule 1 contains the forms to be used for the purposes of applications, notices and other communications required by Part 4, Division 1 of the Act.

PART 3—FORM OF DECLARATION BY PARISH OFFICE HOLDERS

3.1 *Declaration by parish office holders*

Schedule 2 contains the form for the purposes of section 20 of the Act.

PART 4—DIOCESAN ASSESSMENT

4.1 *Amount of diocesan assessment*

The annual diocesan assessment is the greater of—

(a) 5% of the base stipend fixed by the Diocesan Stipends Committee under the *Diocesan Stipends Act 1991*; or

(b) an amount calculated as the sum of—

    (i) 11 per cent of the first $60,000 of the total net assessable income of the parish; and

    (ii) 16 per cent of so much of the total net assessable income of the parish as exceeds $60,000.

4.2 *How total net assessable income calculated*

The total net assessable income of a parish is the total assessable income less permitted allowances.

4.3 *Meaning of total assessable income*

(1) Subject to this regulation, the total assessable income of a parish comprises—

    (a) all money given to the parish, including money given through offerings, collections and planned giving;

    (b) all money given to the parish in donations;

    (c) an amount (other than a negative amount) that represents the gross income from fundraising less any expenses in the year that the expenses were incurred;

    (d) general bequests, legacies and trusts at the time when they are expended to the benefit of the parish;

    (e) interest received;

(f) dividends received;

(g) an amount (other than a negative amount) that represents the gross income from property less any expenses on property income in the year that the expenses were incurred;

(h) 50 per cent of the net proceeds from the sale of shares and other tangible and intangible assets at the time of realization;

(i) the proceeds from the sale of land and buildings that are not subject to Diocesan policies relating to the sale of property;

(j) an amount (other than a negative amount) that represents the gross income from fees, use agreements and the sale of goods or services, less any expenses in the year in which the expenses were incurred—

except for—

(k) money received from donations and fundraising for payment out to Christian mission outside the parish and to Christian welfare agencies and Christian charities;

Note: moneys collected or otherwise received by a parish for payment to a welfare agency, charity, government agency, municipality or other organization that is not Christian form part of the parish's assessable income even if 100 per cent of the funds received are remitted to the entity on whose behalf the funds have been collected or received.

(l) donations received for payment into a building fund investment account with the ADF to support a building fund approved by the Archbishop in Council;

(m) donations received for and paid to one of the Funds of the Melbourne Anglican Foundation;

(n) income from fundraising for a specific cause where—

    (i) the specific cause has been widely promoted to people outside the parish;

    (ii) all the net proceeds are remitted to the specific cause; and

    (iii) there is written evidence that the Archdeacon is aware of the fundraising activity and the specific cause;

(o) specific bequests, legacies and trusts invested in a special trust account in the ADF that allows the funds of the account to be expended only for a tightly defined purpose;

(p) interest on building funds, bequests, trusts and opportunity shops approved by Archbishop in Council;

(q) the proceeds from the sale of land and buildings that are subject to Diocesan policies relating to the sale of property;

(r) grants received from the Government of Victoria, a municipal council or a corporation;

(s) grants received from the Diocese, from the Melbourne Anglican Foundation or from another parish;

(t) other receipts such as payments received from insurance claims, payments for long service leave, deposits and security bonds, reimbursement of expenses incurred, transfers between accounts, business activity statements, tax receipts;

(u) loans received.

(2) For the purposes of regulation 4.3(1)(b) the donations that form part of the total assessable income include—

(a) money received from; or
(b) money expended for the purposes of any capital works of the parish or for the repair, maintenance or improvement of any buildings, grounds, equipment, systems, amenities or other assets of the parish by—
an opportunity shop which is conducted by the parish or which is a trust or corporation referred to in section 41(2) of the Act.

(3) For the purposes of regulation 4.3(1)(e) and (f) interest on and dividends from funds in an approved building fund, bequest account with the ADF, ADF reserve account or opportunity shop investment account do not form part of the total assessable income until paid to the parish.

(4) For the purposes of regulation 4.3(1)(g)—
(a) the expenses associated with property income include a proportion of the costs associated with holding, maintaining and operating that property corresponding to the hours of use in generating income relative to the hours when the property is available for use; and
(b) all the property of the parish may be treated as a single portfolio for the purposes of calculating expenses.

(5) A net loss on the sale of shares or other assets is not a permitted allowance, but during the two financial years following the financial year in which the loss was incurred it may be off-set against any net proceeds to which regulation 4.3(1)(h) applies.

(6) For the purposes of regulation 4.3(1)(k) and 4.4(1)(e), a payment is considered to have been made to a Christian welfare agency or to a Christian charity only if—
(a) the payment or donation is unconditional;
(b) the agency or charity is not connected to the parish

and does not perform work or services for the parish or provide work or services to the parish; and

(c) the agency or charity is not a trust or corporation referred to in section 41(2) of the Act.

4.4 Meaning of permitted allowances

Subject to this regulation, the permitted allowances are—

(a) the total amount of any stipend, salary, salary sacrifice, motor vehicle allowance, housing allowance, superannuation, corporate card, long service leave and sickness and accidence insurance paid by the parish from assessable income to or in respect of curates;

Note: an amount paid to a curate from a grant is not paid from assessable income.

(b) the total amount of any stipend, salary, salary sacrifice, motor vehicle allowance, housing allowance, superannuation, corporate card, long service leave and sickness and accidence insurance, up to a total amount of $3500, paid by the parish from assessable income to or in respect of students undertaking Supervised Theological Field Education;

Note: an amount paid to a student from a grant is not paid from assessable income.

(c) in respect of all clergy and authorised stipendiary lay ministers who are not referred to in paragraphs (a) or (b) and who are not—

(i) the vicar;
(ii) acting during the absence of the vicar or during a vacancy in the incumbency;
(iii) involved with youth;
(iv) involved with benevolent causes—

50% of the first $100,000 paid by the parish by way of stipend, salary, salary sacrifice, motor vehicle allowance, housing allowance, superannuation, corporate card, long service leave and sickness and accidence insurance, and 25% of any additional amount so paid, except to the extent that the amount so paid has been funded by grants from the Melbourne Anglican Foundation that have not been matched by donations to that Foundation by or through the parish;

(d) the amount represented by G in the following formula—

$$G = C - (P \times 1.03)$$

where

C is the amount of the total assessable income referred to in paragraphs (a), (b) and (c) of regulation 4.3;

P is the amount of the total assessable income referred to in paragraphs (a), (b) and (c) of regulation 4.3 in the preceding financial year.

(e) amounts paid by the parish council from the funds of the parish for Christian mission outside the parish;

(f) subject to regulation 4.3(2), amounts paid by the parish council from the funds of the parish for Christian charities and welfare agencies;

(g) grants given to another parish in the Diocese as part of a programme approved by the Archbishop;

(h) money given by the parish to support Christian chaplaincy in schools or universities;

(i) the whole of the amount, up to an amount of $2000, expended on the maintenance of each local worship centre in the parish or paid into a designated account with the ADF for expenditure for maintenance in future years, except for an amount paid into that account in a previous financial year and expended in the current financial year.

4.5 Annual statement of income and expenditure

The income and expenditure of a parish must be given to the

Registrar by 15 December if it is a business day (or otherwise by the next following business day) setting out the information in regulations 4.2, 4.3 and 4.4. The parish must provide that information in the form of an Excel° workbook if the Registrar provides the parish with such a form for that purpose.

PART 5—KEEPING AND INVESTING FUNDS

5.1 Institutions for keeping parish funds

For the purposes of section 34(2) of the Act the ADF and the Melbourne Anglican Fund are prescribed institutions.

5.2 Investing surplus parish funds

Surplus parish funds may be invested in a manner determined by the parish council on the recommendation of the churchwardens, but only if the investment—

(a) is prudent;

(b) is consistent with the fundamental beliefs and principles of the Christian church and the good name and repute of the Anglican Church; and

(c) does not involve investment in a company that has major business activities in gaming, the manufacture of tobacco products, the manufacture of alcoholic beverages, uranium mining or the manufacture of armaments.

PART 6—AUDIT AND INDEPENDENT EXAMINATION

6.1 Form of reporting of irregularities by auditors

The form of reporting of irregularities by auditors is Form 1 in Schedule 3.

6.2 Form of reporting of irregularities by examiners

The form of reporting of irregularities by examiners is Form 2 in Schedule 3.

6.3 Independent examiner to examine accounting thresholds

The independent examiner must verify that—

(a) the total receipts of the parish in the relevant financial year do not exceed $250,000; and either

(b) the electors of the parish have, at the annual meeting of the parish, at their option, appointed the independent examiner; or

(c) the parish council has appointed the independent examiner to fill a vacancy.

6.4 Independent examiner to understand the parish

The independent examiner must obtain an understanding of the parish's organization, accounting systems, activities and nature of its assets, liabilities, incoming resources and application of resources in order to plan the specific examination procedures appropriate to the circumstances of the parish.

6.5 Independent examiner to document the examination

The independent examiner must record the independent examination procedures carried out and any matters that are important to support the factual findings contained in the independent examiner's report.

6.6 Independent examiner to compare accounting records

The independent examiner must compare the accounts of the churchwardens with the accounting records of the parish in sufficient detail to provide a reasonable basis on which to decide whether the accounts are in accordance with those accounting records.

6.7 Independent examiner to review accounting records

The independent examiner must review the accounting records of the parish in order to provide a reasonable basis for the identification of any material failure to maintain those records.

6.8 Independent examiner to use analytical procedures

(1) The independent examiner must carry out analytical

procedures to identify unusual items of disclosures in the accounts.

(2) Where concerns arise from those procedures, the independent examiner must seek explanation from the Treasurer.

(3) If, after following those procedures, the independent examiner has reason to believe that in any respect the accounts may be materially mis-stated then additional procedures, including verification of the asset, liability, incoming resource or application, must be carried out.

6.9 Basis for independent examiner's findings regarding the accounts

The independent examiner must carry out procedures to provide a reasonable basis on which to reach a factual finding that the accounts have been prepared in accordance with the Act.

6.10 Independent examiner to review accounting policies, estimates and judgments

(1) The independent examiner must review the accounting policies adopted and consider their conformity with relevant accounting concepts, consistency of application and their appropriateness to the activities of the parish.

(2) The independent examiner should consider and review any significant estimate or judgment that has been made in preparing the accounts.

6.11 Independent examiner to enquire as to governance and disclosures

The independent examiner must enquire of the Treasurer as to material conflicts of interest, contingencies, internal controls and financial activities that may require disclosure in the accounts.

6.12 Independent examiner and the annual report of the churchwardens

(1) The independent examiner must compare the accounts to any financial references in the annual report that will be presented by the churchwardens to the annual meeting.

(2) The independent examiner must identify any major inconsistencies and consider the significance that those matters will have on a proper and accurate understanding of the parish's financial report.

6.13 Independent examiner's report

(1) The independent examiner must review and assess all conclusions drawn from the evidence obtained from the examination and consider the implications on the report to be made by the independent examiner.

(2) If the independent examiner has cause to make a statement on any matter that has arisen, then the independent examiner must ensure so far as practicable that the report so made gives a clear explanation of the matter and of its financial effects on the accounts presented.

PART 7—PARISH REGISTERS

7.1 Form of parish registers

(1) Each register must be in one or both of—
   (a) a bound book of durable paper and (except in the case of the register of marriages) with each page headed with the name of the parish or congregation, the diocese and the year and information recorded in columns corresponding to the matters to be recorded;
   (b) an electronic register maintained for the purpose by the Diocesan Registry.

(2) Despite sub-regulation (1), this regulation does not require a parish to commence maintaining a bound book in a form required by this Part until all available entries in any previous book relating to the same subject matter have been filled.

(3) An entry in a register must be made promptly following the service or other event to which it relates.

7.2 Form of register of baptisms

The register of baptisms must record—

(a) the next consecutive number of the entry in the registry;

(b) the date on which the person was baptised;

(c) the candidate's date of birth;

(d) the candidate's full name;

(e) the first name and surname of each of the candidate's parents (if known);

(f) the occupation of each of the candidate's parents (if the candidate is aged under 18) or of the candidate (if the candidate is aged 18 or older);

(g) the first name and surname of each godparent;

(h) the candidate's residential address;

(i) by whom the baptism was performed.

7.3 Form of register of children admitted to communion

The register of children admitted to communion under the Canon for the Admission of Children to Holy Communion 1981 must record—

(a) the date of admission;

(b) the name of each child admitted;

(c) the name of the vicar;

(d) the signature of the vicar.

7.3 Form of register of confirmations and receptions

The register of confirmations and receptions must record—

(a) the next consecutive number of entry in the register

(b) the date and place of the candidate's birth;

(c) the date and place of the candidate's baptism;

(d) the date of the confirmation or reception;

(e) whether the service was confirmation or reception;

(f) the names of the sponsors or presenters;

(g) the signature of the confirming or receiving bishop.

7.4 Form of register of marriages

The register of marriages must be in the form of the official certificate of marriage in Form 16 of Schedule 1 of the Marriage Regulations 1963 of the Commonwealth of Australia.

7.5 Form of registers of funerals and burials etc

(1) The register of funerals and memorial services must record—

(a) the next consecutive number of the entry in the register;

(b) the name of the person;

(c) the age of the person;

(d) the residential address of the person;

(e) the date of the service;

(f) the date, place and nature of any other service, rite or action in connection with the disposal of the mortal remains of the person that is known to the person completing the entry in the register;

(g) the signature of the person performing the service.

(2) The register of burials and the interment of ashes must record—

(a) the next consecutive number of the entry in the register;

(b) the name of the person;

(c) the age of the person;

(d) the residential address of the person;

(e) the date of the service;

(f) the date, place and nature of any other service, rite or action in connection with the death of the person that is known to the person completing the entry in the register;

(g) the signature of the person performing the service.

7.6 Form of register of public worship

The register of public worship must record—

(a) the date of the service;
(b) the day in the calendar of the church or, if there is no day, the day of the week;
(c) the hour of the service;
(d) the form of the service;
(e) the signature of the person conducting the service;
(f) the total number attending;
(g) the number of communicants;
(h) the number of those attending under the age of 16 (whether or not receiving communion);
(i) the signature of the preacher (if not the person conducting the service).

PART 8—PERIODIC PARISH REVIEWS

8.1 *Data required in periodic parish reviews*

A periodic parish review must consider at least—

(a) For each of the past five years:
  (i) The number of parishioners;
  (ii) The number of parishioners added to the roll;
  (iii) The number of baptisms;
  (iv) The number of confirmations;
  (v) The income of the parish and the sources of that income (and in particular whether it is from the giving or fundraising activity of parishioners or from other sources);
  (vi) The proportion of income of the parish paid as income or fringe benefits to clergy and lay ministers licensed to the parish;
  (vii) The solvency of the parish;
  (viii) The ability of the parish to fill parish offices and other lay leadership positions;

(ix) The number of parishioners who have offered for ordination;
(x) The number of parishioners serving as missionaries within Australia or overseas;
(xi) The average number of hours per week in which parish buildings are used for parish activities;
(xii) The average number of hours per week in which activities of a missional, educational or fellowship nature organized by the parish take place (such as bible study, house groups);
(xiii) Achievements against the parish's Mission Action Plan.
(b) At the time of review:
(i) Whether the buildings and grounds are properly maintained;
(ii) The parish's ability to meet its Diocesan assessment;
(iii) The parish's risk management plan.

SCHEDULE 1
FORMS RELATING TO PARISH ELECTORAL ROLL

APPLICATION FOR ENROLMENT ON PARISH ELECTORAL ROLL

PARISH*	
Full name:	
Postal address:	
Email address:	
Parish or Authorised Anglican Congregation in the Diocese of Melbourne in which currently enrolled:	
Worship centre for enrolment (in multi-centre parish):	

* or Authorised Anglican Congregation

I declare that—

   I am 18 years of age or older

   I have been baptised

   I am a member of the Anglican Church of Australia

   I do not belong to any religious body which is not in communion with the Anglican Church of Australia.

   I seek to be entered on the parish roll of this parish, and wish to be removed from the roll of the parish in which I am currently enrolled.

   I do / do not *(delete as applicable)* consent to details of my postal address and my email address being on the parish roll exhibited prior to statutory parish meetings and available for inspection by parishioners.

   Signed ....

   Date ....

NOTICE OF REVISION OF PARISH ELECTORAL ROLL

Parish of ……………………………………………

The parish electoral roll of this parish will be revised by the parish electoral committee commencing on ………. [*insert date*].

The *Parish Governance Act 2013* provides that parish electoral roll is to contain the names of people who are of at least eighteen years of age and who—

(a) are baptised;

(b) regularly and habitually attend public worship at a worship centre in the parish;

(c) have signed an application seeking to be included on the roll and declaring that:

    (i) they are a member of the Anglican Church of Australia or of a church in communion with the Anglican Church of Australia;

    (ii) they are not a member of any church which is not in communion with the Anglican Church of Australia; and

    (iii) they are not on the parish electoral roll of any other parish or any Authorised Anglican Congregation in the Diocese other than a roll from which they wish their name to be removed.

The parish electoral roll as revised will be displayed prior to the annual meeting. A person must be on the parish electoral roll to vote at the annual meeting.

A person may apply to be on the electoral roll at any time. A person wishing to apply to be on the electoral roll before the next revision may obtain a form from me at the address shown below and must return the completed form to me before the above date.

    Dated:

    Signed: ……………………………………

    Parish Secretary

    Address:

NOTICE TO CANCEL ENTRY IN ANOTHER PARISH

To the Secretary of the Parish of ....

.... [*name*] of ....
.... [*postal address*] has applied for enrolment on the parish electoral roll of this Parish and has asked for their name to be removed from the parish electoral roll of your parish and it is requested that their name be removed accordingly.

Signed ....

Parish Secretary, Parish of ....

Date ....

Schedule 2
Form of Declaration by Parish Officers

PARISH*	
Full name	
	Date of most recent election or appointment
Office(s) held — churchwarden	
member of the parish council (other than churchwarden)	
member of the incumbency committee	
a member of the vestry for the worship centre of	

* or Authorised Anglican Congregation

I have been appointed or elected to the above office or offices and declare that I am qualified for that office under the provisions of the Acts of the Synod of the Diocese of Melbourne, that I am not a disqualified person within the meaning of the *Parish Governance Act 2013*, and that I will faithfully perform all the duties of that office or those offices and conform to the Acts of the Synod in relation to those duties.

Signed:

Date:

Schedule 3
Forms to be used in Reporting Matters of Material Significance

FORM 1: REPORT TO THE REGISTRAR BY THE AUDITOR

I……………………………… being the auditor of the accounts of the churchwardens for the
Parish of ……………………… report to the Registrar the following matters that have become
apparent to me during the course of the audit or review, namely,

(a) I am aware of circumstances that I have reasonable grounds to suspect may amount to:

> (i) a failure in a significant respect of any of the treasurer, the churchwardens or the
> parish council to comply with a provision of the Act;
> Particulars of circumstances [set out details]
>
> (ii) dishonesty or fraud involving a loss of parish funds or a risk of loss of parish funds;
> Particulars of circumstances [set out details]
>
> (iii) a breach in a significant respect of the terms of any special trust to which property enjoyed by the parish is subject.
> Particulars of circumstances [set out details]

(b) that information or explanation to which I am entitled has not been afforded to me.
Particulars of circumstances
[set out details]

……………………………………………

     Auditor
     Date

www.ingramcontent.com/pod-product-compliance
Lightning Source LLC
Chambersburg PA
CBHW020108020526
44112CB00033B/1100